TRANSFORMING YOUR LIFE

Published by BooxAi
ISBN: 978-965-578-677-4

Transforming Your Life

Conversion — It is a Process

Rebecca D. Montgomery

DEDICATION

I dedicate this book to my book to my mother, Mercedes Williams, and my grandmother, Pearlie Garland Kilpatrick. I also dedicated this book to Mother Charlotte Rosier, a great soldier in the Kingdom of God. These great people helped to shape and mold me into who I am today. May my grandmother and Mother Rosier rest in peace.

PREFACE

God originally had a plan for man when He designed him. From the beginning of time, God created mankind to live in harmony and peace. He intended for all people to build up a strong relationship and with a bond of love. One that would be lasting. God Himself is love.

God is the one who forgives humans for their sins and gives them salvation --if they convert and change over to Him. Man is not always faithful. However, on the other hand, God is always faithful and just. Once a transformation has been made in a person's life then they can begin to see what God will truly do for them. God will enter into a covenant with His people for His name's sake.

These people because Satan stronghold has been destroyed by God. You will be able to tell Satan to take his hands off you. You will be able to say boldly— **I Belong to God.**

Foreword

To make an ordinary change does not get a person in the Kingdom of God. A person simply cannot mix their principles and morals with the activity of religion. A person must be saved. In the book of Isaiah, God tells us that He is the one who will be the one to save, give man help, and restore their souls. Nothing and no one else can do so because no one else has the authority or the power to do so.

In the world today, people are looking for a quick fix or alternative for all solutions. There is no quick fix or alternative. God is the only fix or solution. There are some who say that we are born, we live, and then we die. These people will have a person to believe that nothing comes after these events. The Bible tells the people different. It gives us a choice—heaven or hell.

The Bible tells us that he that livest in pleasure is dead while they live. A life that has been used up for pleasure, pain, or experience will eventually become useless or vanity. Vanity means to be completely empty and being apart from God. It is a life that has no meaning or purpose. The life that has been lived in obedience to God will have everlasting and eternal significance. The foolishness of pride will lead to nowhere.

Contents

What is True Conversion?

Jesus says, "Except you be converted and become as little children, you shall not enter the kingdom of heaven" (Matt. 18:3). Jesus made it noticeably clear that if a person of this world is to be accepted into the kingdom of heaven, that person would have to be converted. In other words, for a person to be converted, it would be a complete necessity to enter into the kingdom of God.

Conversion involves turning from the structure of the world and its anti-God principles. It will consist of turning from dead religion and self-righteousness. A complete change of your heart and mind in order to go in through the narrow gate that leads to life. A spiritual conversion thoroughly changes the path of a person's life. It is not a partial change at which point a person can straddle the fence between two completely different worlds. Unlike sanctification, conversion is not a gradual change that happens over a time period. Rather, it is an actual conversion that happens much deeper inside the soul of an individual. It is a critical decision to break away from the old pattern of sin and the world and embrace a new life in Christ by faith.

This spiritual conversion is so deep that it consists of many alterations in an individual's life. This involves a changing of the mind, which is a mental change, and a change of view, a new perception of God, self, sin, and Christ. It consists of a change of your conscience, which is an emotional change, a change of feeling, a sorrow for sin hh uh committed against a holy and just God. It consists of a change of will, which is a free will change, a willingness to turn away from sin and turning to God through Christ to seek forgiveness. The complete individual—mind, affections, and will—is thoroughly, totally, and entirely changed or converted.

Speaking from a theological point of view, transformation (regeneration) and conversion have two sides of the same coin. Transformation is God's sovereign action by the Holy Spirit in the soul of someone who is spiritually dead in sin. Transformation is the application of a new life in the soul. Transformation gives the gift of repentance and faith. On the other hand, conversion is the AGHB of the one who is transformed. Dr. D. Martyn Lloyd-Jones, a renowned British pastor said, "Conversion is the first exercise of the new nature, increasing from old forms of life and starting a new life. It is the first action of the transformation soul in moving from something to something." Transformation continues and conversion is the result. These two events have a cause-and-effect between them. Transformation is the cause, and the effect is conversion. In other words, transformation is the root and conversion is the fruit.

To declare true conversion, suggest that there is false conversion as well. To put it plainly, there is such a thing as non-saving faith. Matthew 7:21 says, "Not everyone that saith unto me, Lord, Lord, shall enter into the kingdom of heaven so everyone who says Lord, Lord, has not entered through the passage of the narrow gate."

Individuals probably will know the truth and could have felt the sorrows of their sins. However, it is a self-centered sorrow over the price concerning what they will pay because of their sins and not how it has provoked the Holy Spirit of God. The leading provoked example of a conversion that is false is found in the Bible is Judas Iscariot. In a fake conversion, there is death to self, not submitting to the lordship of Christ, one does not have the fruit of repentance-there are only empty words, shallow feelings, and unfruitful religious activities. On the other hand, with true conversion, sin is hated, the world-renowned ego crushed, using your faith, surrendering yourself, exercising faith, Christ seen as precious, and the cross welcomed as an individual's only saving hope. The whole reason for conversion is to bring people into a right relationship with the Heavenly Father. For this reason, Jesus came and died upon the cross for us. It was God who was "In Christ, reconciling the world unto Himself" (II Cor. 5:19). Conversion is the crying need of the soul. Until a person's life changes from a life of sin to Christ, nothing else matters.

It is not simply a change in one's behavior. However, it goes much deeper than one's behavior. It is a change in the very core of a person's life. The changes are so drastic that the Lord and His prophets call it a rebirth, a change of heart, and a fire baptism. The Lord told us in his word to marvel not that all mankind. Yeah, men and women, all nations, kindred, tongues, and people must be born again; yea born of God, change from their carnal and fallen state, to a state of righteousness, being redeemed of God thus, becoming His sons and daughters; and thus, they become new creatures.

"For this reason, they become new creatures; and unless they do this, they can in no wise inherit the kingdom of God" (Mosiah 27:25-26). Conversion just does not happen overnight. It is a process. It only comes from the result of making efforts to live righteously to follow our savior, Jesus Christ. Exercising our faith in Christ is one of these efforts. Another one is repenting of our sins, a willingness to be baptized, not catching the Holy Ghost as some people have said to me on occasions. You cannot catch the Holy Ghost as some would say, even preachers. Some people make Him sound as though people are catching a virus or something. You receive the Holy Ghost, and last but not the least, an individual in faith, endure to the very end.

Conversion being extremely miraculous, and a life changer, it is such a miracle. It is not because one can see or have visitation of Angelic beings and other extraordinary occurrences in what causes one to be converted. I see them on occasions. I only became converted after I fasted and prayed. "Alma also had visitations from Angelic beings; he only became converted after he fasted and prayed" (Alma 5:46). Even Paul saw Christ's resurrection, "He saw within His teachings that no man can say that Jesus is the Lord but by the Holy Ghost" (1 Corinthians 12:3).

You can investigate the Book of Mormons and find that it does provide descriptions of individuals who are converted to the Lord. They genuinely wanted to be good. It was declared by the people of King Benjamin, "The Spirit of the Lord Omnipotent has wrought a mighty change in us, our hearts, that we have no more disposition to do evil, but to do good continually" (Mosiah 5:2). Alma spoke about individuals who, "Could not look upon sin save it were with abhorrence" (Alma 13:12).

They do not fight against the Lord. It was the Mormons who were brave enough to tell a group of Laminities who had been wicked and bloodthirsty but were, "Converted unto the Lord" (Alma 23:6). Not only did these people convert over to righteousness but they went so far as to change their names to Anti-Nephi-Lehies. "They laid down their weapons and stopped fighting against God and their brothers" (Alma 23:7).

They went about sharing the gospel. Enos, Alma, the Elder, Alma, the younger, the sons of Mosiah, Amulek, and Zeezrom dedicated themselves to preaching the gospel after they became converted to the Lord (Enos 1:26; Mosiah 18: 27: 32-37; Alma 10:1-12; 15:12).

After Christ's resurrection, he paid a visit to the people in the Americas. After his visitation, the people were filled with the love of Christ. They all converted unto the Savior on all the face of the land, the Nephites and Lamanites. This ended all animosity and fighting that was among them. Afterward, every man dealt fair and just with one another.

There was no more hatred in the land, because of God's love which was in the hearts of the people. All jealousy and strife, lying, murdering, and all matters of lasciviousness were destroyed. The people just could not be any happier with each other after the hand of God paid the people a visit, there were no more robbers, murderers, nor were there such people as Lamanites, or any other manner of ites. They united and became one in the Lord thus making them heirs to the throne of God (4 Nephi 1:2; 15-17).

Each of them, and they did not have to wait, gave praise, and tarry, was filled with the Holy Ghost as well spoke in tongues as the Spirit of God gave them utterance. Paul asked, have you received the Holy Ghost since you believed? He did not tell them he had come to pray for them so that God would pour out His Holy Spirit on them. The Holy Spirit had been poured out ever since the day of Pentecost. This is found in the Book of Acts chapter 8. The Apostles in Jerusalem, when Peter and John were sent to Samaria to perform hands Philip's converts so they too, can receive the Holy Ghost. They were not sent to tarry and wait on God for the Holy Ghost.

Most are very familiar with the name Jesus Christ. But do all of us know what he taught while he was here on earth? Do the people even know or think about what his mission was? Do they even know what makes his true followers different from any other groups or denominations? Who truly represents Jesus Christ?

In Scripture, Jesus said, "The Greek word "church" translates in the Bible is ekklesia. Its meaning is an assembly, or more accurately, "a calling out" or "called-out" ones. Vine's Complete Expository Dictionary of Old and New Testament Word tell us ekklesia is from ek, "out of" , and Klessis "a calling" (kaleo, "to call"), and was used among the Greeks of a body of citizens gathered to talk concerning the affairs of state, Acts 19:39", "Assembly").

When we look at the Book of Hebrews, we find that it gives a description of this body. This body is described as a body of believers as "The general assembly and church of the first born" (Hebrews 12:23). You will notice that Paul in I Timothy 3:15 the pillar of truth.

Introduction

People go about singing how they have changed. What are they talking about exactly? We experience that conversion means to change, but what will they change from and what will they switch into? This is what I have discovered.

The word conversion has been heard of more so in the circle of the religious world than anywhere else. People frequently talk about how they were converted or their spiritual rebirth. Examples of spiritual change, let's say, changing one's life. By that, I would mean changing from a life of sin and turning it around and converting one's life by becoming a saved person, etc. (for example, a change of heart). Becoming selfless, less judgmental, and demanding. We should humble ourselves more, have more compassion, be more patient, and charitable. Not to be so harsh but to be more peaceful. We should conduct ourselves in a more orderly way, being honest, and generous as the Lord would have us to be. We renovate our minds and hearts as we renovate our society. Thus fore, opening ourselves to spiritual renovation. (change religion to Christianity) For example, an Atheist is a person who does not believe in God. The Ancient Jews, for example, believed that although there are many gods, only one should be served y-h-v-h. Judaism, today, believes in a monistic faith. Meaning that there is only one God. They believe in what they call the Ten Statements, meaning the Ten Commandments. Hinduism, for example, is the third largest religion. It is quite often considered to be a polysynthetic faith, meaning this is a religion that does not worship only one deity but many. "Theists are people who believe in the one true God.

So, what does it all mean to make a transition? (Transition is a context that is usually practiced in Christianity.) It represents a change in one's life from one way of belief to another, from a shallow understanding of something to a deeper one, from not believing to believing. According to one of the definitions in the dictionary, deep is profound. When looking at the definition of profound in the dictionary, it means to enter deeper into subjects of thought or knowledge or having an insight or understanding.

In contrast, being shallow indicates that people are only on the surface or they are lacking or missing the knowledge they need to fully understand. Therefore, if someone says that the people are deep in the meaning of this, they have a profound insight and understanding of Christianity. Meanwhile, having a shallow understanding means that the education on Christianity is only at the top of the surface and the people have a lack of insights. The people who have a profound understanding will be able to connect with Christianity. Shallow people will not be able to have that connection until they can better understand and have the insights they need.

So, what does all this mean for people who desire to change and how they fit in with people of the world and society? And how can people be deep instead of being shallow people?

The origins of the word "spiritualitas" come from the Greek noun pneuma, which means spirit. More and more, "spirit" in its initial perspective is not the opposite of the "physical" or "material." However, of "flesh," or everything that is not of our Heavenly Father. For that reason, an individual who is spiritual, in its initial Christian sense, is merely an individual inside whom the Spirit of God dwells. Even so, is this all there is to conversion?

There are a few who use the word conversion as a definition of just about any righteous change in their life for the better in their personal struggles. However, there are times when people mistakenly believe they were, in fact, influenced by God, Himself.

God has given us the assurance that we have an incorruptible guidance, the capacity to determine between what is good and what is evil. Our Heavenly Father will not pressure us to do good, nor can the devil pressure us into doing evil. So, when it comes to the thoughts of man, the devil only has as much influence as you are willing to freely give him. It was the Prophet Joseph Smith who said, "Satan cannot seduce us by his enticements unless we in our hearts consent and yield." He also stated that the devil has no power over us only as we permit him. In God's Word, he inspires us to embrace life. This is done by reading the Word of God and listening to the voice of God. God does not force himself on us; instead, he comes to us in a calm, still voice. God is not slack when it comes to any of his promises that he has made. The Lord is not slack concerning his promise, as some men count slackness; but is long-suffering to us-ward, not willing that any should perish but all should come to repentance (Deut. 30:19). Genesis 1:26 says, "God created humans in his image and likeness, giving them the capacity to display qualities such as love and justice, and the ability to determine their future." God's Word does not contain a particular verse that tells us that God will not force himself into your lives.

The devil does not truly know what you are thinking. He can just offer you temptations and enticements (the thing you desire the most). However, it is up to you to choose whether you will follow the influences of Satan. If you choose to follow the influences of the devil, he gains stronger power over you and the temptations get much stronger. By the same standards, if you are powerful enough to resist the evil that he sends your way and choose to do good in the sight of the Lord, then you will be strengthened and richly blessed. Unfortunately, this is not the case. Individuals could convert and do constitute a change without the influence of God. Nevertheless, it does not describe conversion as it is depicted in the Bible.

If the religious background was not present, individuals understand conversion since the dictionary provides a reason for the word, denoting a variety. Converting something means changes are created in some sort or another.

The word conversion, from a scriptural standpoint, clearly is considering a modification. The terminus is merely found in one passage of the Bible. For example, the Scriptures tell us that both Paul and Barnabas traveled to Jerusalem, crossing over into Phoenicia and Samaria, teaching the Gentiles. As a consequence, the people showed appreciation and the delight of the Lord was found throughout Phoenicia and Samaria (Acts 15:3). Conversion comes from the verb "convert," which is used in the Revised Version, "return" Psalms 51:13. In another case, the King James Version uses the figure of a verb convert also. You will find in James 5:19, the term "convert," and "converteth" is used in 5:20. The term converts is used in Isaiah 1:27. Other examples, nevertheless, in the Revised Version use the phrase "turn" Isaiah 6:10. In Luke 22:32 and Acts 3:19, Isaiah 60:5c; Matthew 13:15; 18:3; Mark 4:12; John 12:40; Acts 28:27 "turn again." According to the King James Version, God's law is perfect and turning from their wicked ways will restore their souls. The law I am speaking of is to repent and be baptized.

Conversion, in the Bible, is represented as a remarkable, life-changing experience, a process that would not be possible if it were not for the intervention of others and the powerful hand of God. Before we start, let me set the stage and make it crystal clear to everyone that God is the one who initiates the process of the transition. The first thing He does is open the minds of the individuals He is reaching out to or giving an invitation to them to convert so they will have the ability to understand the Scripture as they read through it. He provides the simplicity and deliberation of conception they would not have been able to achieve otherwise.

Normally, this breathtaking and amazing procedure starts when God begins reaching out to the individual(s) who can hear Him or read His truth and accurately explain it as only a true servant of God could. God has the attention of the servant, and He is now able to start to reveal and give an understanding of the true gospel of Jesus Christ.

Immediately the people can have a sense of what the significance of the Holy Scripture of God is to them. An ikon of the Bible becomes full circle and those people whom God allows to be fully converted can begin to unravel the Holy Bible. This is a miracle calling from God indeed.

"God is the one who encourages man to choose life" (Deuteronomy 30:19). Take note that God does not push Himself on anyone. God leaves it up to the individual to make the right decision. As a warning, there are big consequences for the selections they make. This shall quickly be revealed as we go along.

Read on and you will study in this book what the Bible teaches on conversion. In contrast to what one might imagine, this is not an outcome that passes only one time with God. Concerning the Bible, you will see that this is indeed a process.

The procedure starts with God's calling. Second, the crucial stage is to repent or come Godly sorrow in your faith. Third, baptism and the receiving of the Holy Spirit. Lastly, moving up to the climax of the return of Jesus Christ, after the dead in Christ shall be resurrected and quickened in their bodies while being furnished with life everlasting. This is the ultimate change, the transformation and transcendence of death to life. Let us start our journey- going straight to the Word of God—for a clarification of this magnificent transformation called conversion.

Chapter 1

Embracing the Power of God

When we read in Acts, we find that Jesus taught the apostles forty days after He had resurrected (1:3). He commanded the apostles to go to Jerusalem and stay until He arrived so they would receive the Holy Spirit on the Day of Pentecost. Ten days later, He showed up. His disciples asked Him if He was getting ready to build His Kingdom upon the earth. This was done shortly before He descended into heaven.

He said, "It is not for you to know the times or the seasons ... but you shall receive power, after the Holy Spirit comes upon you" (Acts 3:7-8). After this, Jesus vanished into a cloud.

Most of the people today are much like the apostles; they wait for some type of additional strength after they become converted. Talk to the teenagers whose parents will be allowed to drive the family, and they will have no problem understanding that they are getting ready to receive real power. When I drove my car for the first time, I knew exactly what it meant. The same is true with an about to be Christian who is waiting to receive God's Holy Spirit at repentance and baptism. Paul wrote to Timothy, "For God has not given us the spirit of fear; but of power, and of love, and of a sound mind" (I Timothy 1:7). Christians, since they have the Spirit of God, they have experienced real power in their lives. Read on further into the verse and it tells us that a Christian shows love or give in their walk, and their behavior demonstrates a sound mind.

The fact that God's Spirit passes down to the sound-minded is proof that God has a desire for Christians to understand their calling, their conversion, and His purpose for them. He desires for His people to be sound in His way. This should, of course, include an understanding of the simple aspects of true conversion.

When Will God Give His Holy Spirit?

Now the real question is how would a person know if they have God's Spirit? How can a person have a sure way of knowing for certain that it has been given to them? Being that this will be the moment of conversion, then when do the Christian become assured that God has placed His Holy Spirit in them? If a person does not have the Spirit of God in them, then only one thing can be true. Those people are not true Christians. Those of them who do not have the Spirit of God inside of them, remember that He will never have them confused as to whether they have the Holy Spirit. A person will know when they receive the Spirit of God.

In the Book of Acts it reads: "Then Peter said unto them, Repent and be baptized each of you in the name of Jesus Christ for the remission of sin and you shall receive the gift of the Holy Spirit" (2:38).

When accepting the Spirit of God, one accepts real repentance and a proper baptism. The remission of your sins includes repentance and baptism. God has forgiven your sins. Now there will be a particular moment when conversion starts. Also, there will be a certain time when God's Holy Spirit will enter the mind and a person becomes a true Christian and God has begotten a new son and a new daughter.

Now one must ask these questions. Can one say that salvation is now completed at this moment in the Christian? Are they not ever able to sin or be wicked, because they know they have been saved? Can they continue with their old life?

Conversion for a real Christian is a gradual process of one growing and being able to overcome and of changing and developing. How will a Christian do this, one may ask. After this process, what does a Christian look like? And now what does this have to do with a Christian's goal with what a Christian is looking to accomplish as their final reward for working so hard to be a Christian for God?

This is Not an Easy Path

Is the path of Christians an easy one? By becoming Christ-like in character, is it as simple as taking a walk in the park? It is most certainly not. Let us go back to the Sermon on the Mount for the answer that Christ gave. He said, "Enter you in at the straight gate: for wide is the gate, and broad is the way, that leads to temptation. Because straight is the gate, and narrow is the way which leads to life and there will be only a few that will find it" (Matthew 7:13-14). There has always been only a few who are willing to pay the price to live this way of life. I must say this is a difficult one.

If you will recall, Christians "run." It takes a lot of effort to run, the labor is extremely hard! A person gets extremely tired and worn out when running. It takes a lot of energy when a person is running. Have you ever watched people run a long-distance race as they were nearing the finish line? I have a set of twin granddaughters, I raised. I used to watch them and their fellow classmates practice running every day, they did the Cross-Country race. Let us just say, that was not an easy task. My grand twins along with their teammates would be so tired at the finish line. Sometimes while they were running, they had to face the challenges of running up and downhill and over broken ground. Running is not an easy task.

Paul himself said, "I press toward the mark of the prize of the high calling of God in Christ Jesus" (Philippians 3:14). In a previous verse, he said he had to learn to forget those things which were behind him and to "reach forth" to the supreme objective that was ahead of him (Verse 13). If runners have pushed themselves throughout a long race, they are completely exhausted in the end. If they should give up before they reach the finish line, they have no chance of winning. Therefore, all his practice and their efforts in preparing for their victory would all be for naught. Anyone who has wrestled will know that wrestling is a very strenuous task. Oftentimes to the point of becoming nauseous and throwing up. Paul also made a comparison with it to fighting. Let us look at I Timothy 6:12, "Fight the good fight of faith, lay hold of eternal life." Paul also talked about Christianity as "wrestling" (Ephesians 6:12). Also, go over and read II Corinthians 10:4, it states, "For the weapons for our warfare are not carnal but mighty through God to the pulling down strongholds (Greek: castle)."

Nothing that concerns war is pleasant or easy. It is, however, destructive and it typically will end with many fatalities. Some would be wounded and others would be killed. This is the reason Paul cautions Christians to "war a GOOD warfare" (I Timothy 1:18). Christ is called the "CAPTAIN" of our "salvation" (Hebrews 2:10). The Soldier that is not experienced or has not trained can easily become a casualty of war if he does not or is not willing to submit to his captain's orders!

What is God's Purpose for Christians?

Throughout the ministry of Christ, He has proclaimed the gospel according to the Kingdom of God. A person can find hidden inside this message that an understanding that is awesome and incredible human potential for anyone who truly relinquishes their whole life over to God. Christ spoke of God's Kingdom as he traveled through the country and hillsides of the earth.

He spoke a lot in parables, however, only a few really heard and understood His message was focused on the coming of the Kingdom's Government, of God that is to come. Oftentimes, when He spoke, He spoke in parables. Sometimes when He spoke it included how true Christians were educating themselves to become a part of God's government.

Reading Matthew 13, we find there are a half dozen "kingdom" parables. This chapter starts out with the parable of the "Sower" and the Seed," describing how a person puts out seeds in different areas and the types of soil it falls upon. The parable describes how the seed had grown and produced in the person so much that they prospered and brought it great fruit, in some cases. There were other cases, where the seed did not grow and prosper as well. The seed either grew on top of the soil and the sun came out, it scorched its roots and died. Or it died before a root could get started. Some who received it, "their character grew. Some thirty-sixty or even a hundred-fold" while they were in the Kingdom.

The third parable describes the Kingdom starting as an extremely small "grain of mustard seed" that grows into a huge tree. After this parable, Jesus describes God's Kingdom as leaven that spreads until the dough has saturated the earth that holds it. The fifth makes a comparison of the hidden treasures of the Kingdom that are found in a field. The one who finds it goes and sells his possessions to purchase this field.

The sixth parable describes how the Kingdom is the pearl that will bring a great price, which an individual purchases only after they sell all that they own to raise the amount of money which they need to purchase it. The seventh parable, which is the final one and the only one found in this chapter, describes the Kingdom as a "net" to catch all types of fish. As a good fisherman picks out the good fish from the bad fish. The fisherman will keep the good and throw the bad away. The bad represents all those who are bound and destroyed by fire.

CHAPTER 2

ALL MUST REPENT

There are many who want to hear a message of repentance. However, a person needs to be told that there are certain dimensions in the realm of the spirit world that can be tapped into when they welcome repentance with open arms. Repentance is when a person changes their mind and turns away from something that is not pleasing to God the Father. In this case, turning away from and changing your mind about sin. We must also humble ourselves as little children. Yes, our mind must be a childlike mind.

In the book of Matthew 18:3, Jesus tells us, "Except ye be converted and become as little children you shall not see the kingdom of heaven."

The higher your desire gets, the more you will start to enjoy the kingdom's message that says repent and be ye baptized in the name of Jesus. You might be thinking, I do not know how to repent. You may start by renouncing sin. You may start with repenting from believing in the sinful nature of this world. Give up lying, cheating, stealing, and whore mongering, just to name a few. Whore mongering does not always mean running after a man or woman while being married to another. It could be that one is whoring after other gods. For example, a person can make money, fast cars, or just a plain car, a child or children, etc., a god.

All these things are not of God and can lead an individual into a life of destruction. Your way or your system of doing things is nothing like God's. "For my thoughts are not yours, neither are your ways my ways saith the LORD," (Isaiah 55:8). You want to put on the same nature that God has. Let the world go and embrace God and a newness of life.

Repentance is not just saying you are sorry or pleading for God's forgiveness; it is changing your mind about something. After repentance, you must align yourself with God.

When we speak about conversion in the biblical sense, we are talking about a drastic change in an individual's life.

Some people think that they have done some things that are so awful in their lifetime that God will not accept them. That thinking is so much further from the truth. If a person is ready to make this important change in their life, then all that person needs to do is repent and be baptized.

People without a background for religious purposes can change. Those people know and understand that conversion is nothing more than a simple change in their lives. Just look up the word conversion in the dictionary and it will tell you that.

When we research the biblical aspect of conversion, we find that it represents a miraculous, life-transforming process. This process is a difficult one to do on one's own. People will need God to intervene on their behalf for the transformation to take place. Without the intervention of God, there is no transformation. To be honest, he is the one who initiates the conversion process. There is no other way.

When this happens, he is calling or giving those people over to conversion so that they can begin to understand the Scriptures with clarity and the depth of wisdom and knowledge that one could not have acquired on their own. The great and miraculous process can in no way happen until God himself enables that person to hear or read, his truth that is accurately explained by servants he has called before them.

God said in his Word to come as you are. He would like for everyone to go to heaven or live on the new earth that is to come. You must be willing to convert over and willing to go the distance.

We can see from reading the verse in the Book of Acts that the believers who were in Ephesus had never heard of the Holy Spirit. However, when Paul came and laid his hands on them, the Holy Spirit came upon them, and they all spoke in tongues. Each of them, and they did not have to wait, give praise, or tarry, they were filled with the Holy Spirit and also spoke in tongues as the Spirit of God gave them utterance.

Paul asked them; have you received the Holy Spirit since you believed? He did not tell them that he had come there to pray for them so that God would pour out His Holy Spirit upon them. The Holy Spirit had been poured out (That was pointed out in Acts 8). The apostles in Jerusalem when Peter and John were sent to Samaria to lay hands on Philip's converts so they too, can receive the Holy Spirit. They were not sent to tarry and wait on God for the Holy Spirit.

Faith and Repentance

It has already been explained that God gives His Spirit at baptism which follows repentance. However, how does a person achieve repentance? Can an individual simply declare it by proclaiming, I have repented? It is not that simple.

Just as a person's initial calling, repentance is a gift from the Father Himself. When it comes to speaking concerning Gentiles coming into conversion, Acts 11:18 says, "Then has God also spoken to the Gentiles repentance unto life?" II Timothy 2:5 talks about experiences where "God" will give repentance to the acknowledging of the truth. Lastly, Romans 2:4 goes into detail that it is the "goodness of God" that gets up to repentance. It is not something the people will work up so that God will give them His Spirit (Acts 2:38). One must seek God, and Him for the gift of repentance. It does not come automatically, and it should never be treated as such. God will grant repentance to everyone who chooses to seek him. However, a person cannot seek him half-heartedly. He must be sought with the person's whole heart as David did in Psalm 51. Read the entire chapter.

You might be asking yourself, "How do I repent?" The Word says, "All have sinned" (Romans 3:23). Next you might ask, "What is Sin?" To answer those questions let us look at I John 3:4. It states, "Sin is the transgression of the law." This refers to the law of

God. When we deal with humans, we deal with the flesh or what you call the carnal minded which is a hostile thing. He or she does not just hear it or talk about it. They live it. "For not the hearers of the law are just before God, but the doers of the law shall be justified" (Romans 2:13).

Therefore, God will only give His Spirit to the one that He has conquered—one who is willing to obey Him (Acts 5:32).

The world would describe God's Law as hard and unpleasant. However, John says, "For this is the love of God, that we KEEP HIS COMMANDMENTS: and his commandments are not grievous" (I John 5:3; Romans 13:10). The Law of God is holy and not defiled, good and spiritual (Romans 7:12, 14) and it is through the Holy Spirit of God that we are able to obey God for that reason alone should cause the humans to practice God's love. Romans 5:5 says, "The love of God is shared abroad in our hearts by the Holy Spirit."

A person who has a mind to repent, has turned from their own way. This person now has a mind to follow God. His authority is now in their life. When a person gets this mind, they will strive to do as Christ does and produce the fruit of the Spirit. Christ speaks about "bearing much fruit." Sometimes later Christ lays on Paul's heart to list all the "fruits" of the Spirit—love, joy, peace, long-suffering, gentleness, goodness, faith, meekness, and temperance (self-control) (Gala. 5:22-23). These fruits are the evidence we produce in our conduct as we are Spirit led—the converted—person.

When a person repents and their mind is turned from their sinful ways, that person no longer has a selfish way of life. A Christian's whole thinking becomes transformed. They have changed completely—to a whole new way of looking at things in their life and at life. Old things are done away with, and all things become new.

These Christians now live by faith (Hab. 10:38; 2:4). This is the faith of Christ, not that of human faith. This is what makes it possible for a person to obey God. The person now must show some type of signs. Then they must be able to show an initial faith that they have been forgiven at baptism (Acts 2:38). At this moment, the Christian's slate—concerning the conduct has been wiped totally clean. Their slate is washed white as snow through the cleaning of the blood of Jesus Christ (Eph 1:7; Col. 1:14). So now the first human faith is replaced by Christ, who is now a converted person (Romans 1:17). We have now seen that faith in one of the fruits of God's Holy Spirit which has entered into the mind of the Christian which begins at conversion and baptism.

Do not get confused! God does not owe us the Holy Spirit just because we choose to practice faith and repentance. The Holy Spirit of God is not something you can get from doing good deeds any more than salvation can be gotten by your works (Eph. 2:8-9).

CHAPTER 3

ALIGNMENT

What is an alignment? After driving a vehicle around for a while over the highways and byways, that vehicle will most definitely need alignment. Alignment has a huge effect on how a vehicle feels when driving, how it handles, and how quickly the tires wear out.

A properly aligned vehicle will feel stable at all times, track straight and true, and it will boost a person's confidence when then presses the gas to go faster in the vehicle, braking and controlling the wheels. If a person is driving a vehicle and it has poor alignment, the vehicle will pull the owner all over the highway, and possibly need constant corrections to drive straight ahead.

After some time has passed, miles, wear and tear, the chassis of the vehicle will settle, and it will bend. It will not be sufficient to just look at it and recognize it. However, it will only take a small fraction of an inch to negatively affect the wheel alignment.

In some sense, sin does the same to a person's life. It is a must to have God in your life and not Satan. He will have your life all out of control. For this, not a person will need to align with God.

So, the question now is, what does it mean to be in alignment with God? Alignment with God—what does it mean? Let us read the Scriptures to see what the Bible has to say about alignment with God. What does it look like to live it out? What are the thoughts on how a person can get in alignment with God in a way that will be most fulfilling to them?

Anytime I hear the word alignment, I think of my truck needing an alignment before my tires go all bald on me. However, this is not the alignment I am referring to, but it works in a similar way. We are the same in terms of getting out of control and an individual's life would be all over the place the same way if their life were in the hands of Satan. However, in the hands of God, a person will be just the opposite. The alignment I am thinking about is the one when a person is aligned with God. Alignment with God is mostly heard about at the beginning of the year. It deals a lot with a person's goals, values, and their purpose. It is referred to sometimes when a group of experiences begin to come together in a confusing yet mystical way. The same as when the stars are aligned. A person may say that they have made so many bad choices and committed so much sin that they fear that God will never forgive them or accept them into His Kingdom. On the contrary, God is a forgiving God and although He knows that not everyone will choose to be in His Kingdom, He still would like for everyone to be in it. God will forgive an individual and continue to love them. The blood of Jesus will cleanse you from all your sins, except blasphemy against the Holy Spirit.

The meaning of alignment is when a set of entities, experiences, or individuals are physically set up in a straight line and fused together to bring about a common objective. For example, when an engine is built and placed inside a vehicle to operate as it was intended. But before that happens, the engine will need components such as a carburetor, radiator, starter, alternator, water pump, you get the idea. For the engine to operate as it was intended, it will need all these components and they must be fused together for it to work.

The same is true with man and God. If your components do not align with God, then you will not be as operational as God intended. Without your mind, heart, and soul being in alignment with God, you will not be able to function as God has intended without those components.

When it comes to alignment in our lives, it means that we are working together with our Heavenly Father so that we may pursue his call and purpose. Like anything else, we can attempt to pursue our own objectives rather than God's and his call. We will not be operating in the manner we were designed or intended to.

Will you be willing to put your life in the hands of Jesus, who can cleanse you from all your sins? Allow the Holy Spirit to lead and guide you out of that sinful life and into righteousness for all of eternity. Come to God and find truth and righteousness and begin your life anew with Jesus today. You will be glad you did. No one wants to burn in hell for all eternity when they leave this world. Won't you give Jesus a chance?

All it takes is for you to come godly sorrow before the throne of Grace and give your life over to Jesus and let Him take control of your life. Remember to believe that Jesus is the true son of God. Confess your sins before God and be baptized. You choose death or life everlasting. Will you come? Jesus is knocking now. Do not let this chance pass you by. This is your time. Will you come? Tomorrow may never come. God is waiting. Jesus has his arm wide open.

Those of you who feel that you are ugly, a nothing, and a nobody and that you will always be a nobody. That is not true. People in and out of your life have told you that you will never amount to anything. Well, do not believe them. Everyone is somebody in the eyes of God. Most importantly, you are loved. And you can come and live in His Kingdom. Surrender to Him right now. You are somebody in God's Kingdom. Man and society put you down because you do not dress like them, or you are different. Man or Society does not dictate your life or tell you who you are. God does.

What Do the Scriptures have to say about being in alignment with God?

In the Bible, you will never actually see the term alignment. It will, in turn, point to the same conclusion as the word alignment. If we want to be in alignment with God, not the other way around. We must put it to work.

When we are in alignment with God, it means that we find our greatest joy and pleasure in him. Reading Genesis 15 we find God speaks to Abram. He tells Abram not to be afraid. He lets Abram know that he is a shield for him, also his great reward. Psalm 37:4 reads, "Delight thyself in the LORD; and he shall give thee the desires of thine heart."

What we find in common with these two verses is that God himself is our result. The goal and the reward which we pursue after. God promises us in Psalm that if we pursue him, we will receive our greatest joy, love, and most of all him.

There was a time when I believed that in order to delight God meant to give up what I wanted for a second rate alternative. Big mistake, with God we are never downgraded, if anything we are upgraded. Anything we give up for him, he will replace it with way more than we can imagine.

Matthew 19:29 says, "He is a God of multiplication and abundance. We are only giving up a cheap imitation or reward and abundance that the world is offering us."

ALIGNMENT WITH GOD MEANS SUBMITTING TO HIS WISDOM INSTEAD OF TRYING TO INVENT OUR OWN

In the Bible, the Book of Proverbs is well known as the Book of Wisdom. This book continues to be that true wisdom that can only be found in God. What he has to offer us is far greater than anything we can attempt to put together on our own.

Proverbs 2:6 says, "Indeed, if you call out for insight and cry aloud for understanding, and if you look for it as you would for silver and for hidden treasure, then you will understand the fear of the Lord and find the knowledge of God."

Proverbs 3:5-6 are similar verses, "Trust in the Lord with all your heart and lean not to your own understanding; in all your ways submit to him and he will make your way straight."

Aligning with God Means Always Becoming More Like Him

There are two verses in the Book of Romans that tell us how we are still in process.

Romans 8:29 tells us, "God predestined us to be conformed to the image of his Son, that he might be the firstborn among his brothers and sisters."

However, Romans 12:1-2 tells us, "Therefore, I urge you brothers and sisters, in view of God's mercy, to offer your bodies as living sacrifice, holy and acceptable to God—this is true and proper worship." Do not conform to the things of this world but be transformed by the renewing of your mind. Then you will be able to test and approve God's will—his good, pleasing and perfect will."

These two verses reveal how we conform—either we become more like Jesus, or we become more like the world. One can easily say that our life's work (our true and proper worship) is to continuously drift back to him, allowing his purpose and plan to mold us, and not us attempting to mold God or circumstances he predestined for us in accordance with our purposes and plans.

When we think about surrendering our life to God it is a huge and scary step, no doubt. Because of who we are we have this strong desire to keep this tight grip on how we understand life, the things and the people around us, our dreams, and our plans.

However, why build a foundation on shaky grounds when we have the **Solid Rock** as our foundation? A foundation that gives us foolproof that we cannot fall with him by our side. We can trust God with our desires, hearts, and understanding in him. He is an unchanging Father and the fact that he will not hesitate to set us straight.

I Corinthians 12 says, "Paul creates a metaphor of the Church as the body of Christ with Christ being the head. Everybody comes together playing their roles to make a whole towards one particular purpose." If one part of the body becomes dysfunctional, for example, it begins to pull away because that part thinks it is better than the rest of the other parts, or have a desire to play a different role, or if the part simply feels it is no longer important and retreats—then we are not operating in a full capacity as we should, or as God intended. For this reason, we are no longer living out the role God established for us.

We all must work together to make a whole. This is our purpose in Christ—and when we all play our parts, what a big difference that will make.

ALIGNING WITH GOD MEANS WE LOOK TO JESUS

Jesus himself set the alignment with God while he walked here on earth among us. He did this for us as the Son of God and still he is equal to God. He put aside his rights, humbled himself, and became obedient, as stated in Philippians 2. Remember, God has never asked us to do anything that he did not do first.

As we read the Gospels, Matthew 26 in particular: "Not as I will, but as you will. You will be done."

We do not do this alone. A perfect example is when Christ went before us and paved the way for us to conform to his image.

Alignment with God looks like delight. Surrender, submission. Humility. Obedience. Conforming to Christ. Playing your role in the church. Thankfully, since Jesus comes down to earth, we are not expected to perform perfectly for God. Remember, Jesus himself said nonperfect, but the Father. In any event Jesus took care of that for us. God's plan and will are already perfect. We do not have to be. We just need to come as we are in the name of Jesus.

Welcome the grace of God on this journey. You can never be fully in tune with God's plan and purpose all the time; you will not always make the "right" decision. We are, as human beings are prone to make mistakes.

However, God still reaches his arms out wide to you. Continue to turn back to him.

CHAPTER 4

CONVERSION

What does it mean to be converted? A great deal of misperception is going on as far as the term conversion is concerned. This confusion has opened a door to serve a great purpose to Satan, the lost souls are blinded. (II Corinthians 4:4)

The hymn writer clarified this misunderstanding when he asked the question, "What can wash away my sins?" He turned around and responded by saying, "Nothing but the blood of Jesus Christ." The only thing that can wash away our sins is the blood of Jesus Christ. There is nothing else that is powerful enough. The attempts of man nor the way man behaves has nothing to do with our salvation. It is our faith that determines our eternal destiny through the shedding of the blood of Jesus Christ-- that is what saves us. When we read Romans 4:5, we will find that salvation is not established because a person does good deeds, has good manners, or does good works. Still, there are those who would sing the verses to the hymn that is mentioned above and simultaneously speak the very opposite of having a flawed interpretation of the doctrine of conversion. They will tell you, for instance, that it is, "Nothing but the blood of Jesus that can clean us up from our sins". However, you must give up your old habits and change your lifestyle to be saved. You have no choice but to convert. A Christian may, possibly, inadvertently teach human works for salvation. This, however, cancels out what the Word of God is saying, "For it is by grace you have been saved, through faith; and you cannot do this yourself; it is the gift of God; Not of works, lest any man shall boast" (Ephesians 2:8, 9).

Having salvation is not contingent upon what we have or have not done. Nor does it hinge upon what we desire or what we do not desire to do. It only depends upon Jesus Christ, who has already died for us on the cross at Calvary. In words spoken by Jesus Christ, "He that believed in the name of the only begotten Son of God" (John 3:18). Notice if an individual is rebuked or not rebuked is established upon whether he or she has faith in or not has faith in Jesus Christ.

What about conversion, though? When does conversion come about? "Be converted!" What does that mean? When does it occur?

The Apostle Peter did not convert until three years following his salvation. A shocker, huh? What effects does this have on the use of the expression "be converted"?

For starters, let us shine a light on Peter's conversion. In comparison, Peter's salvation did not take place until after Jesus had been baptized by John the Baptist. Peter was led to Christ by his brother Andrew. "He findeth his own brother Simon, and saith unto him, We have found the Messiah, which is being interpreted, the Christ. And he brought him to Jesus" (John 1: 41, 42). However, the conversion is spoken of only after Christ established the Lord's Supper and just prior to Jesus passing into the garden of Gethsemane, on the eve prior to his crucifixion. Read Luke 22:32, "But I have prayed for thee (Peter) that thy faith may not fail; and when thou art converted, strengthen thy brethren." Peter did not truly convert until after the resurrection of Jesus Christ. This was only due to the nature of his Christian lifestyle and NOT his salvation. Three years had passed from the time when Peter put his faith in Jesus Christ as his Savior and found salvation. Peter gave a testimony sometime later that the way we live has nothing to do with our salvation. Reading from the Amplified Bible, I Peter 1: 18,19, "You must understand that you were delivered from the unproductive way of living inherited from our forefathers, not with corruptible things, for example, silver or gold, but you were bought with the precious blood of Chris the Messiah, like that of a sacrificial lamb without blemish or spot."

The phrase, be converted, is it not also used for salvation. You would be correct if you answered yes. Jesus said in Matthew 18:3, "Verily I say unto you, Except you be converted, and become as little children, ye shall not enter the kingdom of heaven." Notice, when discussing salvation, Jesus is not simply telling us to be converted. Jesus paused and clarified what He meant when he said, "Be converted" when dealing with salvation. He said, "Except you be converted and come as little children."

In other words, Jesus explained what he meant by conversion, by salvation, to be a person who is an adult to humble themselves as a little child to be saved. What are we being taught by this? A little child must depend upon its parents for everything for them to sustain life. In the exact manner Jesus is said to have salvation, you must totally depend upon Him for everything and His death for us on Calvary to be saved. What is it that can completely clean me up from all my sins? The answer is, "Nothing but the blood of Jesus!"

In addition, Jesus said, "But whoso shall offend one of these little ones which believe in me" (Matthew 18:6). Christ was talking about the little children whose salvation came because of their FAITH in Him. An adult must understand that they will have the same faith as a child to be saved by Christ.

The epistrophe is a Greek word meaning to revert, to turn again, has only been interpreted once "convert," once converteth, and six times converted. The epistrophe is a Greek word that means reversion, revolution, and is changed once to the term twist, to be precise, to turn quiet around or reverse is interpreted once as "conversion."

When we read James 5:19,20, it mentions saved people being converted. It starts out with "Brethren, if any of you..." The Christian who goes astray, being converted, would be saved from the penalty of their sins and perhaps prolong their lives here on earth.

You will find in the Scripture, Matthew 13:15; Mark 4:12; John 12:40, and Acts 28:27 where each discusses the people who are lost and have walked away from the Word and cannot see it. They have a need to "be converted" and get back to reading the Word of God, which covers the Gospel letter in which they are to have faith to receive salvation.

Correspondingly, Acts 3:19 talks about those who confess that they trust in the Word of God, even though they deprived of, disowned, and slain Messiah, the Son of God, whose real personality was made known to the prophets in the Scriptures, read Acts 3:18. The individuals who are lost are required to renew their minds for the remission of their sins, and "be converted," get back into the Word of God, have faith in it and be familiar with the Bible that the Christ that they sent to slaughter was without a doubt, their Messiah.

To demand a conversion that is sound consists of a mandate for a transformation in behavior either in the direction of the LORD or human is an additional component of works or man's attempt at the scripture of grace. And if by grace, consequently, it will no longer be any more works: if not, there is no more grace. However, should it be of works, then grace will be destroyed for good: or else, work will vanish as well (Romans 11: 6).

Repent

The second step, which steer in the direction of transformation of life. You will find in Romans 2:4, "Do you show contempt for the riches of His kindness, tolerance, and patience not realizing that God's kindness leads you toward repentance?"

First, we believe in God; second, repentance. However, you might be asking the question, are you positive that God will forgive me? Your answer is found in I John 1:9, "If we confess our sins, He is faithful and just and will forgive us our sins and purify us from all unrighteousness." You can also read it again in Exodus 34:6-7, "The Lord, the Lord, the compassionate and gracious God, slow to anger, abounding in love and faithfulness, maintaining love to thousands, and forgiving wickedness, rebellion and sin."

So, as you can see, the LORD takes better care of us than we deserve to be. Yes, God wants to forgive us. John 3:16 says, "For God so loved the world that He gave His one and only Son, that whoever believes in Him shall not perish but have eternal life."

This is what God's love and His goodness cause Him to do for us. Therefore, we must believe in God first. Then we must come to the knowledge that we are sinners and repent. "Repent, then, and turn to God so that your sins may be wiped out," Acts 3:19

If the people are not for their sins, then no one is about to repent. We will find in 2 Corinthians 7:9, "Now I am happy, not because you were made sorry, but because your sorrow led you to repentance." Repentance is basically being godly sorry for your sins, and you stop doing those sinful things. It is not in sorrow because you have a fear that you will be punished, but because we should hate sin because we realize that it grieves God's heart if we hurt for the sins that are here on this planet. Is that something we do naturally for ourselves, to repent? The answer is no. When we read Acts 5:31, "God exalted Him to His own right hand as Prince and Savior that He might give repentance and forgiveness of sins to Israel." We have heard, "Repentance is being so sorry for sin that you quit sinning."

A bridge has been strengthened across the great Zambezi River in Africa. It is located just below Victoria Falls, a large bridge extending over the ravine over the most terrifying turbulence of the waters on this planet. Built by engineers who work their way from both sides of the river. They stretched it out across a single distance to each of the two supports to meet up in the middle, therefore putting the finishing touches to the bridge.

Repentance and belief are the supports of the bride that allow us to pass over from earth to heaven. They come together to make salvation possible for us. You cannot have one and have enough. You need both. We must have faith in the LORD, and we must repent. It is a waste of our time to attempt to be Christians if we do not repent of our evil doings. We will not be able to transform ourselves from sinners to Christians any other way. In Jeremiah 13:23, we read, "Can the Ethiopian change his skin or the leopard its spots? Neither can you do good who are accustomed to doing evil." Repentance is essential. Not repenting is one of the reasons we do not have happiness in our lives. A great deal of people incorporate a form of Christianity and not now, nor have they ever really repented. Thus, has not ever experienced happiness in their Christian walk. This is the reason why many spiritual staffs do not ever hold rivals since they have not repented of their sins—they still have not been converted. Friend, have you repented? Will you repent?

Confession

After repentance, the next step to becoming a Christian is confession. "Confess your sins to each other and pray for each other so that you may be healed," (James 5:16) "He that conceals his sins does not prosper, but whoever confesses and renounces them finds mercy," (Proverbs 28:13). Confession that leads to the denunciation of sin is the true type. Additionally, however, is there anything else that is needed on behalf of the repentant sinner? "If the wicked gives back what he took in pledge for a loan, returns what he has stolen, follows the decrees that give life, and does no evil, he will surely live; he will not die," (Ezekiel 33:15).

True repentance and confession do not merely mean to quit sinning. However, to do everything necessary to correct any wrongdoing that individual has done in the past. An individual can not merely steal money and have the anticipation that God will forgive them for it unless that individual attempts to return that money that they took. If not, it would not be true repentance or true confession.

Once an individual has really repented and confessed, our Heavenly forgives, we have read in 1 John 1: 9, "If we confess our sins, He is faithful and just and will forgive us our sins and purify us from all unrighteousness." Forgiveness is God's work, not ours. Once we confess, we merely start to have the faith that our

Heavenly Father forgives us, and He does. You now have a clean sleight.

Walk in the newness of your life. At this point, you may or may not think that sins have disappeared, but they are. Do not depend upon what you are thinking or feeling, simply believe that God has cleansed your soul.

The son of a priest made a point to sustain a life away from a godly path. Rather, he embraced a life of corruption and sin. His name became famous in the affairs of the world; however, he had a slip up and went to his lowest state. When he gave his testimony, he communicated that he was a drunkard, a drug addict, and a person who was just down and out. However, after fifteen long years, he decided to give that life up and give God an opportunity to deliver him and he was magnificently converted. Afterward, he returned home only to discover that his poor dad had died of a broken heart, calling his name, and over those fifteen years he was not there, his mother kept a lamp in the window every night and all night.

People, God has kept a light in His window for each of His disobedient children, and while the light is still burning, the drifting sinner might come back. Will you return at this moment, for God will forgive you? There are three crucial steps: To have faith that God will deliver us from our sinful ways, repent, and confess our sins.

CHAPTER 5

BAPTISM - WHAT DOES BAPTISM REPRESENT?

Jesus' death, burial, and His resurrection from His grave. Instead of rising of the grave. It means letting the world know about the faith an individual has in Christ and after they have been immersed in water and come back up, they will not be the person who went down into the water. The old man dies. A new person comes up and their life begins anew. The individual's life is no longer characterized by their sinful action but brings about a new life with Christ just as He resurrected into new life.

To be baptized does not mean that an individual is on the same level as salvation. However, it exhibits a portrait of salvation.

Think of it as a ring when it is used to represent a marriage. You might take the ring off your fingers, but you will still be married; but with the ring being on your finger, it lets the world know that you are in a committed relationship.

You are now new in your salvation, and baptism is a representation to those who are watching you and to those you will communicate with later that you are no longer a slave to sin and death but is alive in Jesus. You can now live in freedom because of who you are in Christ.

Read Romans 6: 3-10.

Did Jesus Get Baptized?

Jesus set an example for us. If you will recall, Jesus was born into this world without sins. He was born of a pure virgin. So, did he need to repent? No, and he certainly did not need to be baptized. As we find in I Peter 2:21, Christ left us an example that is so we could follow his steps. If you will notice that example was left in Matthew also, "And Jesus when he was baptized, went up straightway out of the water." The remainder of this verse has a recording of Jesus' symbolic acceptance of the Holy Spirit as in the form of a dove descending upon Him. As this event is taking place, a voice from heaven is saying this is my Son whom I am well pleased. True Christians are the sons and daughters of God. May God be as pleasing with all of us as we continue to seek to overcome the temptations of the sin that Jesus overcame!

Baptizing by the Authority of Christ in His name

You might be asking yourself why do we have to be baptized in the name of Jesus? What does it mean to be baptized in the name of Jesus? The Royal Canadian Mounted Police used to shout, "Stop in the name of the law," when they were running after someone. Whenever a policeman would shout to someone to stop in the name of the law, that person knew that means to stop by the authority (the power, the office) of the law. God is the supreme authority and His law. To certain actions Christ will assert his authority. Baptism is one of them.

The Bible says that Jesus baptized more people than John the Baptist ever did. Did you also know that the Bible says that Jesus did not baptize anyone? How can the two statements be true? If you take a closer look, you will see that Christ had His disciples to baptize many people.

John 3:22, for example, "After these things came Jesus and His disciples into the land of Judea; and there He tarried with them and baptized them. This verse clearly states that Jesus was baptized." One other example 4:1, "When therefore the Lord knew how the Pharisees had heard that Jesus made and baptized more disciples than John, (though Jesus Himself baptized not one but His disciples)."

This scripture is an important one. Why is it important? How can Christ Himself baptize so many people when it clearly states that He baptized no one? This was the very reason that Christ Himself had indeed authorized His disciples to baptize on His behalf –in His name—and God agreed with the baptizing. It was still as though Christ did the baptizing because His disciples were doing it in His name. They did it all for Him, in the sense that they were acting under His authority—and this is considered as though Jesus did it Himself.

Christ tells us Christians, "Whatever you shall ask in my name, that I will do" (John 14:13) and "If you ask anything in my name, I will do it" (Verse 14). Note: These two successive verses carry the weight, what Christ said in both is the same thing. When Christians receive the answers to prayer, it is the result of them praying in the name of Jesus. John 16:23 makes it so plain all can understand: "And on that day you shall ask me nothing..." Whatsoever you shall ask the Father in my name, He will give it to you. Hitherto to have you asked nothing in my name (Verse 24). You must understand that if we come to Him by the authority of Christ, the Father who sees you in Jesus' name will answer your prayer. There were cases where it has been said that Christ did appoint Christians as power of attorney on His behalf in their prayers. By doing so, Christians are authorized by God to perform many tasks in His name.

Baptism, God Commanded It

We have established that Peter commanded repentance followed by baptism. Let us now take a few moments and look at Acts 17:30, "And the times of this ignorance God winked; but now commands all men everywhere to repent and be baptized." This is something that everyone must do. God commanded this.

Christ Himself gave a command to his disciples to baptize the people so that they may be saved. He joined salvation and baptism together. He made it a condition of what Christians must do to receive eternal life. His disciples have always practiced baptism when a new convert receives Christ. Act 2:41 says, "Then then they that gladly received His word was baptized." Acts 8:5 says, "Then Phillip went down to...Samaria... But when they believed Philip preaching the things which concerned the kingdom of God" (if you will notice, this is the exact same message that ties to what new converts must believe) and in the name of Christ they were baptized. You will find some people who will say that this was a mere "Baptism by the Holy Spirit," (Verse 15-16). This causes this to be an unlikely analysis, for the reason that when Peter and John "When they came down the prayer that they may receive the Holy Spirit (for as yet it was fallen upon none of them: only they were baptized in the name of the Lord Jesus.)"

If the baptizing of these new converts was a simple baptism of the Spirit of God, then how could it be said in the Bible that people were baptized when the Spirit of God had not fallen upon any of them? This would not make any sense unless baptism and accepting the Holy Spirit of God are two separate events, as stated in Acts 2:38!

According to Acts 10:44,47-48, a compelling statement was made concerning the command for someone to be baptized properly. God used Peter to give the first sermon to the Jews, speaking on baptism in Acts Chapter 2. God used him again ten years later (in 41 A. D.) to become the first apostle to preach the gospel to Gentiles. Sometime later Paul was chosen to be the apostle to the Gentiles. Cornelius, a devout man received the gift of the Holy Spirit (10:45). This was rather a unique experience for this reason in advance of the Holy Spirit, thus receiving the Holy Spirit. Peter responded immediately with this question: "Can any man forbid water that should not be baptized...?" And he commanded them to be baptized in the name of the Lord. This is plainly a commandment to be baptized in water!

The Great Commission of Christ Includes Baptism

It was started early on that Christ gave a direct command to His disciples to baptize. Notice also in the gospel of Mark when Christ's Great Commission to His disciples, "And he said unto them, Go you into all the world and preach the gospel to every creature. He that believeth and is baptized shall be saved; but he that believeth not shall be damned" (Mark 16:15-16). One cannot be saved if they only believe, a person must be baptized as well.

Matthew 28:19-20 also bears a record of the same instruction commanded by Christ; however, it adds points and leaves out some that Mark does not. Both records have the same Commission, so they each must be accepted together. The record of Matthew, "Go you therefore, and teach all nations. Because this was mentioned in Mark, this had to include the teaching of the gospel of the Kingdom of God. The verse did not stop there; it went on to say "baptizing them in the name of the Father, the Son, and the Holy Spirit: Teaching them to observe all things whatsoever, I have commanded you." In his Great Commission to his disciples, the Word states it so plainly that Christ himself commanded baptism!

It is important to realize that this Scripture explains that baptism is done in the name of the Father, the Son, and the Holy Spirit. Instead of being the word "in," it should be properly translated "into." While Acts 2:38 only says to be baptized "in" the name of Jesus Christ, Matthew bears a record of using a longer phase. Are these two scriptures in conflict with each other? Can it be broken or inaccurate—sometimes by one other scripture? According to John 10:35, it cannot. This is not possible. The Bible will never contradict itself.

Baptizing in Jesus' name and being baptized into the Father, the Son, and the Holy Spirit are two distinctive points. Discussed first was the issue of authority to baptize on behalf of Jesus Christ —a person will either have or will not have the authority to baptize. The concluding discussion is the issue of being baptized into the Family—the Godhead of the Father, of the Son, and the power of the Holy Spirit. Although this book is not intended to address this issue, it must be realized that this is not referring to the unbiblical doctrine of the trinity, which rejects the very definition of the Kingdom of God. Centuries after Christ had built his Church—the trinity first appeared as teaching in the great false "Christian" church in the third century A. D. It was brought into the church as a fake substitute to take the place of the truth that God is making his Family much bigger.

What Is the Right Mode of Baptism?

What is the way God wants us to be baptized? Does He want us sprinkled, poured, or immersed? Christians must not only follow God's command to be baptized, but baptism must be performed in the way God has commanded. Otherwise, the baptism will not be validated. It would be as though it never happened.

We must ask ourselves what does the word baptize mean? Does it mean to sprinkle? Does it mean pour? To find the answer to these questions we must first take a closer look at the Greek word used wherever the words baptism and baptized are in the New Testament.

First, it is extremely important that we make a mental note that the word baptize is really a Greek word. It is not an English word. The readers must be made aware that the New Testament was written first in Greek and then it was translated into the English language. Baptize is a word that represents a departure from design of the translations in 1611, the same time the King James Bible was translated. The translators, when they came to the word baptized, they made a choice not to translate it. Had they translated it, the proper way to baptize would be to immerse, dip, or put into. The English word pour comes from the Greek word Cheo and the word sprinkle comes from rantidzo. God Himself chose the word baptize for the reason he did not want sprinkling or pouring to represent the correct symbol of conversion. Second, let us just consider the issue in this way. When a person is being sprinkled or pouring water on them, they cannot be immersed. One can only be immersed if one is being immersed.

God is a spirit that says what He means and means what He says, "No wonder when John the Baptist was baptizing people, he went and picked out a certain area." Because there was a lot of water in the place where he picked out (John 3:2). There would not have been any reason to sprinkle or pour. The same with Philip and why he was baptizing the Ethiopian eunuch it says, "They dip them down into the water... and he baptized him. And when they come up out of the water..." (Acts 8:38-39). This verse does not consist of simply using a bowl full of water to sprinkle or pour over someone's head. Lastly, it is as well, not awfully hard to see the reason for Matthew 3:16 write it down after Christ had been baptized, "Went up straightway out of the water."

None of these verses are consistent with either the sprinkling or the pouring. The simple pattern of the Bible is that baptism is a whole lot of water because people are required to go into the water and then come up out of it.

REAL REVIVALS BROUGHT ON BY GOD

Did you ever pray continuously for something year in and year out and did not receive a reply from our Heavenly Father? I am hoping for your answer to be yes to this question because if yours is not, it merely means that you are not a person who prays much. If you spend a great deal of time praying, then you have prayed to God for things you haven't got yet.

One prayer that a Christian who is committed should be praying for that is not answered yet is a prayer for God to send a real revival to our nation. It is still an unanswered prayer since nothing comes close to a revival in modern times to the many instances of true revival that the LORD has sent in the years past. Real revival is not simply hanging a banner or putting a sign saying a revival is happening here at this church nightly this week beginning at 7:00 p.m. Real revival is no quick-fix arousing reply that results in a short-term encounter. However, there is no long-term fruit of righteousness.

Real revival is when the living God sovereignly and mightily breaks down the past of man with the great news of His salvation. It always starts with the people of God coming under the profound condemnation of evil and turning away from that evil in true repentance. It is consistently composed of renewal biblical truths, particularly the truth concerning how sinners are brought together with a holy God. Thus, it also includes a renewal of the centralization and conviction of the Word of God over our lives. The transformation of the Heavenly Father's presence, power, holiness, and truth expectedly overflows from the church and into the world, consequently causing many conversions.

If I Continue to Fall, What Then?

As new Christians, we were told that once we had accepted Christ into our lives, we have been cleansed from sin and we are no longer a slave to sin. In other words, God has forgiven us of all sins that we have committed in our lives. So why must we pray? We pray for forgiveness of our sins if we are now saved. If a believer, why is it that they have to continue to ask God to forgive them of their sins, because God has already forgiven them of all their sins. We are talking about the past, present, and future. Have those believers lost their faith in the promises of God since they are asking Him for something He has already given them?

To some degree, this is a true statement. When we read the Scriptures, we find that it teaches us not to request that God give us saving forgiveness after he has already given it to us once.

Why do you and others Rejoice When You Get Baptized?

The people rejoice to accept a new person in Christ into the family of God.

After you have accepted Christ's gift of salvation, and God accepts you as His child, the house of worship becomes a family of believers who desire to welcome you in the exact way as they would a newborn baby as it makes its entrance into the world by its mother and father. Being a follower of Christ is not something that we are meant to do on our own. The House of Worship is a pillar to lean on, support you in a time of need, to pray for you, and to assist you in finding out what step you should take next. As you place yourself around other individuals who love Christ, your faith will develop. You will notice Christ works in you as well as through you.

A few of your family members and acquaintances might not understand your decisions to follow Christ and to be baptized, but it will be alright. As you continue to take steps in your walk with Christ, those individuals in your life will notice the transformations that are being made by God in you. One of the better methods to continue rejoicing in the goodness of the Heavenly Father is by telling your story of how you were converted and how Christ is transforming you.

It no longer matters what you did in the past or your present, you have a place where you belong. You have become a part of the family of God and He is just beginning with you. Now, that is truly worth rejoicing over.

Read Ephesians 2:18-22.

CHAPTER 6

THE COMING OF THE KINGDOM OF GOD

Christ said in the Sermon on the Mount, "But seek you first the Kingdom of God, and His righteousness" (Matthew 6:33). As a Christian, you must always strive toward these two familiar objectives. If you notice, the first preference is to seek the Kingdom of God. However, he has to grow in righteousness, "In My Father's house are many mansions...I go to prepare a place for you, I will come again, and receive you unto Myself; that where I am, there ye may be also" (Matthew 14:2-3).

Take note that Christians are not going to be with him—in heaven or any place else—because Jesus said, "I will come again." (Heaven was not the reward of the saved. Christians have been offered an inheritance of leadership over the Earth (Matthew 5:5).

In another chapter 15:1-2, Christ went on to say, "I am the true Vine...every branch that bears fruit, He purges it, that it may bring forth more fruit." In Verse 5, he reiterates it, "Bring forth much fruit," and as you read a little further Verse 8 says, "Herein is My Father glorified, that you bear much fruit." Lastly, He says, "I have chosen you...that you should go and bring forth (Verse 16.) A Christian will bear fruit in their life. Verse 8 continues to say, since you have done this, "so shall you be My disciples."

Christ identifies you as his disciples and begotten sons and daughters of God by whether you bear fruit in your life!

We must consider a few essential verses concerning the Kingdom of God.

The pre-flood of God's servant Enoch (the great-grandfather of Noah) also preached concerning the Kingdom of God. Jude recorded a description of this message, "And Enoch also… prophesied…," saying, "Behold, the Lord comes with ten thousands of His saints, to execute judgment upon all," (Verses 14-15).

Daniel wrote the same, "But the saints of the most High shall take the kingdom and possess the kingdom forever," (7:18). In Verses 22 and 27, he again states that this reward is for the true Christians.

In the Book of Revelation, it is recorded in multiple places where Christ, through John, makes offers of the Kingdom to those who overcome. Take note, "And he that overcomes, and keeps My works unto the end, to him will I give power over the nations: and he shall rule them with a rod of iron," (2:26-27), and "To him that overcome will I grant to sit with Me in My throne," (3:21).

Lastly, take note of Revelation 20:4-6, talking concerning the saints, which says, "And I saw thrones, and they sat upon them… and they shall be priests of God and of Christ, and shall reign with Him a thousand years." When combined with Revelation 5:10, "It is apparent that the saints that are resurrected become both kings and priests," who reign on the earth with Christ.

This news is certainly unique and priceless. The world does not have a clue concerning God's coming Kingdom, which Jesus will set in place when he returns. "The god of this world," (II Corinthians 4:4) has deceived mankind (Revelation 12:9). Christians are in training on a daily basis. Thus, it is extremely important that they have a good understanding of their "leadership" practice.

It has already been clarified that God gives His Spirit at baptism, which follows repentance. The next question is, how does a person achieve repentance? Can an individual simply declare it by proclaiming, "I have repented? Is it just that simple?" The answer to all these questions is no. It is not that simple.

Just as a person's initial calling, repentance is a gift from the Father Himself. Whenever it comes to speak concerning Gentiles coming to conversion, Acts 11:18 says, "Then has God also to the Gentiles granted repentance unto life." I Timothy 2:25 talks about experiences where "God "will give repentance to the acknowledging of the truth. Lastly, Romans 2:4 goes into detail that it is the "goodness of God" that brings us to repentance. The Holy Spirit is not something that God just hands out to people. His Holy Spirit is a gift (Acts 2:38).

One must seek God and Him for the gift of repentance. It does not come automatically, and it should never be treated as such. God will grant repentance to everyone who chooses to seek him. However, a person cannot seek him half-heartedly. He must be sought with that person's whole heart and soul as David did in Psalm 51. Read the entire Psalm at your convenience.

You might be asking yourself—how do I repent? The Word says, "All have sinned and come short of the glory of God" (Romans 3:23). Next you might ask, what is sin? To answer those questions, let us look at I John 3:4. It says, "Sin is the transgression of the law." This refers to the Law of God. When dealing with humans, we deal with the flesh or what you call the carnal mind which is a hostile thing (Romans 8:7). People will just naturally refuse to obey God. They cannot help that it is a fatal flaw in humanity. Human nature will find a way to disobey and break God's Law. However, a true Christian will not break the Law of God and make it a point to obey Him. Christians do not just hear it or talk about it—they live it. "For not the hearers of the law are just before God, but the doers of the law shall be justified" (Romans 2:13).

"Therefore, God will only give his Spirit to the one that he has conquered—one who is willing to obey him" (Acts 5:32).

The world would describe God's Law as hard and unpleasant. However, John says, "For this is the love of God, that we KEEP HIS COMMANDMENTS and His commandments are not grievous," (I John 5:3, Romans 13:10). "The Law of God is holy and not defiled, good and spiritual," (Romans 7:12) and it is through the Holy Spirit of God that we are able to obey God and for that reason alone cause the human to practice God's love. Romans 5:5 says, "The love of God is shed abroad in our hearts by the Holy Spirit."

A person who has a mind to repent, has turned from their own way. This person now has a mind to follow God. They are surrendering all to God—surrendering to his government, his authority, in their life. When a person gets this mind, they will only strive to do as "Fruits of the Spirit." Christ speaks about "bearing" much fruit. Sometime later, Christ lays on Paul's heart to list all the "fruits of the Spirit"—love, joy, peace, long-suffering, gentleness, goodness, faith, meekness, and temperance(self-control) (Galatians 5:22-23). These fruits are the evidence we produce in our conduct as we are Spirit led—the converted person.

When a person repents and their mind is turned from their sinful ways, that person no longer has a selfish way of life. The thinking of a Christian then becomes transformed. They have changed completely—to a whole new way of looking at things in their new life. Old things are done away with, and all things become new to them.

"These Christians now live by faith," (Hebrews 10:38, Habakkuk 2:4). This is the faith of Christ, not that of human faith. This is what makes it possible for a person to obey God. The person now must show some signs. They must be able to show an initial faith that they have been forgiven at baptism (Acts 2:38). At this moment, Christin's slate beforehand concerning the conduct has been wiped completely clean. Their slate has been washed as white as snow through the cleaning of the blood of Jesus Christ (Ephesians 1:7, Colossians 1:14). So now the human faith is replaced by Christ, who is now a converted person (Romans 1:17). We have now seen that faith in one of the fruits of God's Holy Spirit which has entered the mind of the Christian now begins—at conversion and baptism.

Please do not get confused! God does not owe us the Holy

Spirit just because we choose to practice faith and repent. The Holy Spirit is a gift (Acts 2:38), as is repenting itself. The Holy Spirit of God is not something you can get from doing good deeds no more than salvation can be gotten by your good works (Ephesians 2:8-9).

Supporters of the Kingdom of God

Concerning the message of the Kingdom, what comparison can be established between true and false Christians?

Jesus declared, "Two other cities I must declare the good news of the kingdom of God because for this I was sent forth," (Luke 4:43). What was the reason Jesus made the kingdom of God the primary topic of his ministry? He understood that with him being the King of that Kingdom, he, including his brothers who were raised from the dead, would take care of sources of the afflictions of humanity starting from the root- wickedness and Satan (Rom. 5:12, Rev 20:10). He later instructed his disciples to make known to men that the Kingdom in anticipation of the completion of the existing practice (Matt. 24:14). Individuals who simply confess to be followers of Jesus do not get involved in this labor- in truth, they are not allowed to. What is the reason for this? There are at least three: First, if you do not understand it, you cannot preach it. Second, many of them have a shortage of compassion and backbone required to stand up to and deal with mockery and hostility that might come because of sharing the message of the Kingdom with their neighbors (Matt. 24:9; I Pet. 2:23). Lastly, false Christians do not have the spirit of God (John 14:16, 17).

In contrast, true followers of Christ have identified with the kingdom of God is all about and what it will bring about. In addition, they present the significance of the kingdom of God's urgency in our existence, declaring it throughout the world with the assistance of God's spirit (Zech. 4:6). Do you do your part in this labor; if so, do you do it on a regular basis? Are you making any kind of effort on your part to make any type of improvement as a Christian to make it known to the world? Maybe, if you make time to spend in the ministry or by being more active in it? There are a few who have tried to make improvements to the condition of their ministry by making greater use of the Word. God's Word is alive, and it bears power, proclaimed the apostle Paul, who made it a practice to make this argument coming from the Holy Bible (Heb. 4:12 Acts 17:2, 3).

When I read John 12, I find that Jesus made a victorious entrance into Jerusalem. As I read my Bible, it mentioned that a whole lot of people took the branches of the palm tree as they went to meet up with him. They also were shouting, "Hosanna! Blessed is He who comes in the name of the Lord! The King of Israel!" (John 12:13). They went down only a few verses later, and a lot of the people stopped believing.

What took place in those few short verses? What changed the mindset of the people so quickly? What was the reason for the multitude to switch up from rejoicing with Christ and recognizing him as King of Israel to walking away from him and then crying out for him to be put to death? There could only be one answer for that. He spoke the truth and it appears that they simply could not handle it. Perhaps they did not accept the love of the truth and that they may be saved (II Thess. 2:10).

However, permit me to ask this question: Are you indeed a lover of the truth? Are you genuinely a true follower of Christ?

Do we desire to have a spiritual awakening and revival in this nation? If we do, we must be lovers of the truth. That means that we cannot break down and compromise with any type of dark forces. As a Christian, he must be strong enough to the point when the way gets too hard for them. They will know to turn to God, pray, and not get weak with any little storm and turn back. It means that they will have to speak the truth with unconditional or agape love regardless of the personal cost. After all, it is what Jesus did. Will a Christian try to be a friend to the world and turn out to be an adversary of God (James 4:4)?

You must not come on too strong or repulsive with the scripture. Christ was never that way. However, Christ did not present a few difficult truths in love. When you read John 12:25, 26, Christ spoke these words, "He who loves his life will lose it, and he who hates his life in this world will keep it for eternal life. If anyone serves Me, let him follow Me; and where I am My servant will be also. If anyone serves Me, him My Father will honor."

Jesus told us in His Word that we should follow him. Christ said, in an instance, where was he going?

He went to the cross. Are you eager to crucify your carnal self to follow, to surrender to the labor of the Holy Spirit in your heart? The Father, Son, and the Holy Spirit expect this of you.

In the early days of Christianity, God spread his gospel through witnesses who had the courage to be followers of Jesus. In the face of unlimited hostility and temptation to go well with it, the church of the early days did not compromise but stood their ground. Today, God communicates to the world through faith, particularly during the time when people are going through their trials. We could take pleasure in our inheritance of how the universe was changed. However, we must keep in mind with regards to the huge challenges and antagonists pre-Nicene followers withstood. The followers of Jesus were not executed simply because they had faith that Jesus was a righteous man. Instead, they were brutally beaten, wounded, and burned; their leaders were **steadfast** and would not bow down to serve any other gods.

Pliny the Younger was a lawyer and a governor of Pontus and Bithynia from 111-113 CE. Anyone whom he interrogated and found guilty because they were associated with the name Christian received the death penalty.

Explaining True Conversion

Take care to remember that the power of the Spirit of God helps an individual to be able to grow and overcome. This power is Jesus living inside of Christians. Without the help of Christ, the new convert will not be able to grow or overcome anything. They will only go downhill fast. When Christ said to us to "Bring forth much fruit" (John 15:5), he followed up with it by saying, "For without me you can do nothing." The physical area. Spiritual problems simply cannot be conquered through our physical, mental, or emotional effort.

In John 15:1, Christ tells us that he is the true Vine. We are the branches. In order for Branches to grow, they must be connected to the Vine. This only happens through God's Spirit working in the mind of a person. Christ also said, "Out of the belly shall flow rivers of living waters. He was speaking of the Spirit, which the people who believe in him shall receive," (John 7:38). As the Spirit performs good works, the Spirit of God flows out of the Christian. Hence, it must be recharged, or it will be diminished and gone completely. For this reason, Christ said, "You know how to give good gifts unto your children. How much more shall your heavenly Father give the Holy Spirit to them that ask Him," (Luke 11:13). You must constantly go in prayer and ask for more of the Holy Spirit.

Paul wrote, "I can do all things through Christ which strengthens me," (Philippians 4:13), and, "My brethren, be strong in the Lord, and in the power of His might," (Ephesians 6:10). Christ also said, "With God all things are possible," (Matthew 19:26). This is only true of you if God's Spirit is actively working and growing inside you!

However, truly profound conversion does not happen overnight. Paul wrote only to learn later the Corinthians were only babies in Christ (I Corinthians 3:1). He gave a description metaphor: they must first learn to roll over, then crawl, before walking, and even then, at first, in a sporadic, toddling style. Spirituality, he will only begin to finally run.

Paul had a great understanding of this. He made a comparison of conversion and running a race (I Corinthians 9:24). Of course, it did not click immediately (win).

This is the Christian way of life. A slow and steady growth through the day-to-day practice which produces progress in the life of the individual who is imitating Christ. Newly Christians truly struggle from the heart to be different—to turn their life around and go in the way of God for the rest of their life.

Chapter 7

Paul Struggle

As we read the Word of God, we will find that it is filled with stories of God's greatest servants fighting to overcome sin. In almost every case, they had to see how complicated and oftentimes extremely hurtful lessons. When researched thoroughly, Moses, Noah, David, Samuel, Peter, and many others are seen to and did fight all types of troubles known to human beings. Paul is a representative of a classic example of how one of the greatest servants fought to overcome sin. At the end of his life, he could say that he had "fought the good fight" and that he had "run his course." Knowing that a crown of glory awaited him. How often did this occur without a lot of wrestling, pressing, running, fighting, and warring against their human nature?

Read carefully Romans 7:14-23. It will teach and encourage you that you are not by yourself as you travel the path to overcoming Satan, society, and self, all of which will lead to sin!

Paul wrote, "For we know that the law is spiritual: but I am carnal, beneath sin. For that which I do not allow for what I would, that do I not; but what I hate, that do I," (Verses 14-15). He proceeded to write, "For I know that in me (that is, in my flesh) dwelleth no good thing: for to will is present with me; but how to perform that which is good I find not. For the good that I would I do not: but the evil which I would not, that I do," (Verses 18-19).

It was almost as if Paul did not desire to do it; his human nature, his flesh, caused him to do exactly the opposite! Why?

The father led him to record the answer for our use: "I find then a law, that, when I do good, evil is present with me...But I see another law in my members, warring against the law of my mind and bringing me into captivity of the law of sin," (Verses 21, 23).

Paul continued to say that only the power of Christ's Mind in him was he capable of overcoming and getting the final victory in maintaining the law of God, rather than obeying the true "law" of sin. Only in this way could Paul later say that he "fought the good fight" and had "run his course" to victory.

Make no mistake. Christianity is an all-out war! However, this is a war the Christians should expect to win—if they continue their path to draw close to God and to receive strength from overcoming. God looks at the intent of the heart. Your overall desire and motivation are important to Him. He has a desire to know if, after you sin, you are sorry, for it will always be determined to strive to do better than we do. He understands the temptations that plague Christians better than we ourselves do. He watches over us to see if we will be sober and vigilant as we root out sin from our lives and if we will continue to press on.

Struggling with Sinful Thoughts

To concentrate on the positive, it would be a good idea to start with the eight steps of Philippians 4:8-9 in the renewing of our mind. A lot of us confront the sinful thoughts in our minds. These thoughts will attack our minds without an invitation.

Maybe you have gone to church, perhaps your song, a song of worship, or heard a sermon from the man or woman of God, and while this was happening a bunch of sinful thoughts began to run through your mind. You begin to wonder, where are these thoughts coming from? Or when you lay down in bed at night, these thoughts start to creep into your mind, and you must battle with them. You attempt to concentrate on the Word of God; however, thoughts of iniquity keep on playing in your mind repeatedly. God has provided another line of attack for us to do battle in your mind. "We demolish arguments and every pretension that sets itself up against the knowledge of God, and we take captive every thought to make it obedient to Christ," (*II* Corinthians 10:5 NIV).

God tells us in His Word to set our minds on the battle-seasoned warrior who is fighting the adversary. These wicked thoughts are not defeated by closing your eyes and hoping they go away. To defeat the enemy, we must confront our fears and battle them head-on.

We must do the identical thing when we confront our sinful thoughts. As a soldier on the battlefield, we must have a plan of action with an urge. Our enemy is the devil, and his only mission is to destroy us.

The point is we need to know the Word of God. If we do not have a knowledge of Scripture, we will not have a way of battling with a debate or pride that enters our minds without permission. For us to be able to recognize an error, we first must have knowledge of God's truth. We cannot make this thought obedient to Jesus if we do not know God's truth.

God's truth must be spoken to the wicked thoughts that enter the mind. This is how temptation sets in. The Angel of Darkness gets us to lie, lust after, or focus on any evil thought to cause us to transgress against God. This is what God has to say in that situation—and you need to be reminded of the truths that are associated with those thoughts of iniquity.

This is the main fight Christ had with the Antichrist at the beginning of the ministry when temptation reared its ugly face. Read Matthew Chapter 4. Christ did not ignore the temptation. He confronted it head-on. He quoted Scripture to combat each temptation.

When sinful thoughts enter your mind, do not attempt to run away from them. Turn and attack them the way Jesus did. God has given you the tools to fight Satan, use them. After you have unmasked what it is you are fighting, start to concentrate on the positive things God has talked to you about in Philippians 4:8. Do not go into combat alone, take God with you.

One other plan you can use to assist you in warring against these sinful thoughts is to be responsible for another godlike individual. Allow them to question how you are coming along in combating these sinful thoughts. You will not need to go into details of what you are warring against. However, you could provide them with a statement on how effective you have been over the last few days.

One of Lucifer's strongest instruments is secrecy. If he could get you to keep these fights to yourself, then he has a great chance of conquering you. You become powerless fighting him on your own, in other words.

Concentrate on Christ

Oftentimes, we are confronted with biting the bullet of a complicated issue and chaos. The grief and disappointment can push us to the brink of losing all hope. They will not just vanish. What can we do when we get into situations that we cannot find a way out of?

A third chief plan of attack for renewing the mind is found in Hebrews 3:1, "Therefore, holy brothers, who share in the heavenly calling, fix your thoughts on Jesus, the apostle and high priest whom we confess," (NIV).

There came a time when I was confronted with a tough ministerial decision. Essentially, there were many others who were deciding, and I was the one who was most affected by the decision. The determination, I thought, was not right and I pleaded with these ministers. They agreed to have a meeting with me, where I was given an opportunity to get my concerns out. However, it was not enough to change their minds.

When I walked out of that meeting, I had an enormous weight and vexation. Rather than going straight back to my office, I made a stop at a park nearby and I sat in that park talking to God concerning my situation. I simply decided to concentrate on the Lord for a moment. At that moment, I decided to set the issue aside in my mind. Not anyone but the Lord and His love, His truthfulness, His authentic reassurance, His compassion were the concentration of my thoughts. He vowed to never depart from me or turn His back on me.

The more I place my thoughts on Him, the better I start to feel. When I made it back to my office, the issue was still there. By placing my thoughts on the Lord, I had forgotten all about my problems and disappointments. I could confront the day with the assurance that the Lord was with me.

A few of the situations we confront just do not have suitable solutions. It is times such as these that we can seek the Lord and we can place our thoughts on Him. The whole ball of wax might be in a messy state-nonetheless the Lord is never in a messy situation or chaotic. He sits on the right hand of God making intercession for us! We must continue to fasten our thoughts on Him.

Your Thoughts vs. Your Action

We cannot stop at our pure thoughts. It is not enough. Philippians 4:9 helps us to go one step further. We must put these thoughts into action. Our words must be spoken kindly and the deeds we perform must be done with kindness as well.

Jonah, a prophet in the Old Testament, demonstrates the need for a renewed mind to influence the conduct of an individual. God commanded him to go to Nineveh and preach the gospel. But he made a bad decision to run from God. His deeds disclosed his need for a renewed mind.

Jonah ended up in the belly of a huge fish and there he stayed for three days. A description of the lesson that was learned was described in a magnificent prayer—Jonah, chapter 2. After that little experience, he decided to get up and go to Nineveh and preach to the city as God had commanded. A huge revival took place and thousands of people repented.

After all this took place Jonah still had an issue in his mind. He was filled with so much anger because God decided to forgive the people of Nineveh—so angry that he wanted his life to end.

Our thoughts are shown by how we act out. In some ways, our behaviors speak much louder than our thoughts. If we tell someone that we are extremely big-hearted, watch what we do in our actions. If our actions send a different message, the way we are living clearly states that our lives are not adding up to God's way of thinking.

Renewing our minds is not an easy task and it may take us all our lives to do it. God has provided some extremely unusual gifts to assist us in this process. However, the actual key to keep in mind—is that this is my mind, and I should take complete accountability for renewing it.

The blessings are amazing that God has given us His word that if we renew our minds—we will be changed, we will be able to examine and support God's will in our lives, and we will encounter His serenity.

Emotions—Do They Manipulate Your Thoughts

When you are feeling emotionally good, and everything is going just fine, do you find that it is much simpler or better to think more clearly and have positive thoughts? On the other hand, in what manner would you respond when you are emotionally down in the dumps, demoralized, not interested, or saddened? These emotions, will you permit them to control your thoughts?

The LORD made a promise to provide His children the, "Spirit of self-discipline." Read II Timothy 1:7. If you have plans to renew your mind, then self-discipline is categorically necessary.

The invitation to an experienced Christian is to chasten your thoughts and your feelings. Christ balanced His life in three areas. They were his thoughts, deeds, and his emotions. To be a Christian you will have to do the same.

"Right thinking" leads to "right actions," which leads to "right feelings." The urgency is essential. If emotions are at the front, then they are in the driver's seat and they will propel you wherever they wish to carry you. There's an old saying, if it feels this good, then it must be the right thing to do. Do not do it. It is a trap!

"Right thinking," guides us in responding with "right actions." The correct emotions might not happen right away; however, they will get there in the end.

Say you will do the test for that when you are feeling great. You should step back to third place in your priorities. The correct thinking is established upon observing every situation from the LORD's viewpoint and then the correct deeds-what would Christ do?

But What if One Sins?

It has been established that every human sins. Should new converts expect to continue to sin after they have been baptized? Will they achieve overnight perfection by simply professing the faith or by performing the act of repentance or baptism? The answer to all these questions is emphatically no. There is a long passage in the Bible that will help a person out about forgiveness and other related issues.

The verse that follows bears many instructions, but only after each of them are read first. Note: And truly our fellowship is with the Father and with his Son, Christ...that your joy may be full. This, in turn, is a message that God is light, and in him is no darkness at all. If we say that we have fellowship with him and walk in the light, as he is the light, we have fellowship one with another, and the blood of Jesus Christ his Son cleanses us from all sin. If we say that we have no sin, we deceive ourselves, and the truth is not in us. If we confess our sins, He is faithful and just forgives our sins and cleanses us from all unrighteousness. If we say that we have not sinned, we make him a liar, and his Word is not in us. My little children, these things write I unto you, that you sin not. And if any man sin, we have an advocate with the father, Jesus Christ the righteous: and he is the sacrifice for our sins (I John 1: 3-2:2).

There are a lot of instructions found here. Get your Bible and let us search the Scriptures one verse at a time.

Verse 3: John, the last living apostle in the Bible, speaking for all the apostles ("we"), discusses that Christians can have a real and true fellowship with each other inside the temple of God.

Verse 4: John's purpose was to demonstrate to the people the true source of the fullness of joy permanently.

Verse 5: The one true God is a representation of light—He "is light" –and those who are fellowshipping with the true God of the Word desire to walk into the light and walk out of the darkness of this world.

Verse 6: These are the first six verses starting with the word "if." When using this word, it is always an indication that conditions are attached to it. In this case, those that include free righteous decisions. A lot of individuals insist that they know God to fellowship with him. However, they neither have a knowledge of him nor do they practice his TRUTH in their lives. He tells us in His Word this plainly makes them liars (2:4).

Verse 7: The Blood of Jesus is an ongoing cleanser for all sins— the errors, mistakes, weaknesses, and flaws of the people who strive to walk in God's truth and in fellowship with others who are true Christians. Even though ordinary, Christians do not have the intention to slip and fall sometimes, when they do, they must get back on track.

Verse 8: This verse is extremely important. All Christians need to know they are sinners. "It has been my experience that we are deceivers of our own selves," (Jer.17:9). This is largely the reason why so many people do not grow spiritually and are not able to overcome as they should. Self-deceit—lying to yourself—is still deceitful no matter how you look at it. By doing so, a person has no place for the truth to dwell within them!

Verses 9 and 10: Verse 9 does not speak concerning the unconverted, carnal—minded individual. For the person who realizes that they are a sinner and confesses them, these verses are self—evident Christ is there to wash away their sins and to clean them up—the real Christians when they have backslid from the light of the true Word of the living God and the Law. Christians must teach themselves how to overcome. The same as learning to play the organ or drawing a beautiful picture, this will not happen overnight. It takes practice and hard work.

Chapter 2, verses 1-2: John exercises the adorable term "My Little Children," since it is how God looks at His begotten sons and daughters. In His eyes, we are all little children. Though it was not the intention of God that we sin, when we do, Christ stands before the throne of God on our behalf. This is called advocate. "As our High Priest," (Heb.4: 14-16), Jesus directly goes to the Father himself and pleads our cause before the Father. He has an understanding of what it is like to battle with and to those who recognize that they need both.

The next four verses in I John 2 give a description of the obedient Christian as a person who keeps the Law of God and strives to walk and live the same life as Jesus did (vs.6). This is a person who keeps "God's Word." Striving not to compromise with anything that goes against the Father. This Christian also always seeks to do that which is right in the sight of the Lord God Almighty.

Remember the words of David when you stumble and oftentimes fall. "The steps of a good man are ordered (established) by the LORD...though he falls, he shall not be utterly cast down: for the LORD upholds him with His hand" (Psalm 37:23-24). The same as a parent lifting or steadying a child, God, on a regular basis picks up and upholds. His children allow this amazing promise of God to be an encouragement to you when you feel discouraged because you have fallen short in the Christian walk of life.

So, You Do Not Wish to Join a Church or Denomination

I am sure that we all know people who say, "I am affiliated with this particular church," "I joined the church," or "I changed to another church." Many people join or change church affiliation each year—thousands do it daily. Can an individual find and join a true church of the living God? Following baptism, what has an individual baptized themselves into? We have not been too long quoted the words from Romans 6:3. Remember, it tells us that we are "baptized" into Jesus Christ. "Christ says, we are to be baptized in the name of the Father, the Son, and the Holy Spirit." (Matt. 28:19).

It cannot be found anywhere in the Bible that we are baptized "into" either a denomination or some specific church organization. However, Hebrews 10:26 says, "Do not forsake the assembling of ourselves together, as is the manner of some is but exhorting one another; and so much the more, as ye see the day approaching." Place some emphasis on this verse. It is certain that you have heard this verse from time to time, especially in the last two years. Still, it is crucial.

It is vital that you understand this! So many people have become so confused because they believe that when they are baptized, it puts them into some corporation when the Bible does not state this. Technically speaking, it is not even legal to baptize into an actual membership in a corporation in most countries.

However, do not misunderstand. The newborn Christians are placed into Christ's Church. A careful explanation is needed to completely understand. In fact, there is only one true church, with each of the others, thus, having been built by the hands of men and is as a result, false.

On average, many churches will not baptize a person who has no plan whatsoever to join their church. This is scripturally incorrect. Why? A real Christian is placed into the church that Jesus Christ built not by the hands of men. Christ said, "I will build My Church," (Matt. 16:18). It is Christ, not man who places the people in the Church, thus building it.

How exactly does a person become a member of the true Church of God? Ordinarily, practically most of the churches are in competition with each other, advertising for members. Does the Word of God teach these practices? Paul said, "For by one spirit we all baptized into one body," (I Cor. 12:13). He also said, "For as many of you have been baptized into Christ have put on Christ," (Gal. 3:27). By placing these two verses together, we recognize that a Christian is baptized into the Body of Christ—not just any church organization founded or built by men of this world.

Quickly, "The house of God, which is the Church of the living God, the pillar and ground of the truth," (I Tim. 3:15) is the Bible's definition of the church as a place where the people can find the truth. Why yes, this also includes the truth concerning the accurate manner of baptism.

This is where the connection between being "baptized into Christ" and being baptized into one body. Signifies baptizing into the real Church of God. This must be clarified. Take into consideration Ephesians 1:22-23. Talking concerning Christ, it says, "And gave Him to be the head over all things to the church, which is His body, the church." This pictures Christ adding individual people into the body of His Church right after baptism! Individuals can join football teams, or social clubs (all churches are just religious, social clubs), but only Christ could place them into the Church that He is building. There is not, nor has there ever been such a thing as an "independent" baptism by any supposed believers who has a desire to exist on his own part from the one place where Christ is working. Christ's real ministry must be involved—must authorize the baptism.

Other verses that describe and talk about the Body of Christ are Romans 7:4; 12:4-5; I Corinthians 10:17; Ephesians 4:4,11-16; 5:30; Colossians 2:17; and the whole chapter of I Corinthians 12.

I must make this completely plain so that no one will miss this tidbit. A person is baptized by the Holy Spirit into the Biblical Body of Christ; however, this Body has been unified, organized, and structured, and exists as the only real Church of God on this Earth—preaching the gospel of the Kingdom of God to all nations (Matt.24:14-28; 19-20). This is the required comprehension of the real gospel—the only one that was brought by Christ, which was referenced earlier.

No one can receive the Spirit of God unless they are baptized. No one can be baptized if they do not repent. Recall God's command is, "Repent, and be baptized, and only then a person shall receive the gift of the Holy Spirit." People might have their traditions (another Bible message), ideas, and methods of baptism or opinions concerning how a person can receive God's Spirit— however, doing it in the way that God has instructed us to do so in the only acceptable way!

Never Delay Baptism

In the New Testament, there are a few accounts illustrating that we must not delay baptism after it is apparent that the believer is repentant and ready. While Paul was still called by the name of Saul, he was to be baptized by Ananias to perform this baptism. Ananias had an immediate reaction once he saw Paul (Acts 22:16). I was, "And now why tarry you? Arise, and be baptized, and wash away your sins calling on the name of the Lord." Paul always remembered this. If you will note, when he was baptized the Philippian jailer with his family, this took place sometime after the night, "And still Paul baptized him the exact hour of the night," without ever placing it on hold for the next day to come (Acts 16: 32-33). If the reader will remember that the Ethiopian eunuch was immediately baptized after Philip counseled him (Acts 8).

It is extremely vital to make a mental note that it is not always possible for a baptism to be performed as soon as is best or ideal. Peter, when he gave his sermon in Acts 2, all the original apostles were there with him and were capable of assisting him immediately in 3,000 baptisms (Acts 2:39-41). While this is the ideal method to do it, circumstances do not always allow it to happen.

When Is a Person Ready for Baptism?

When should an individual make the decision to move forward with their baptism? When are they ready for this step? How is it determined and by whom? All these questions are very important and must be taken into consideration. There are some groups who believe that a particular probationary period should be in place so the person can show that they have a clear understanding and have a basic knowledge of being prepared for baptism. Some basic knowledge is required. However, this book has already established and demonstrated that Christians, "Grow in grace, and in the knowledge," for the rest of their lives (II Pet. 3:18). This is not a requirement to gain or acquire before you get baptized. After baptism, the Christian will gradually attain a good amount of knowledge, actually!

Matthew 28:9-20 has already been read, "Repentance, belief of the gospel and being taught all things that Christ has commanded are ascended in preceding an accurate baptism." Then, after receiving the gift of the Spirit of God, Christians struggle to develop and go through the assistance of the Holy Spirit. The Holy Spirit reveals the truth, cleanses, corrects, and renews the minds while continually teaching individuals to move and move concerning the way to freely allow Christ to live His life in them.

The Bible tells us that the Law of God is, "Holy just good" and "spiritual," (Rom.7:12,14). While many people believe that God's Law was maintained by Christ for us that He eliminated—true Christians are starting to understand more profoundly all through their lives that God's Spirit is important to be capable of maintaining the Spiritual Law of God. It is through the Spirit of God that we can understand his will, his mind. And yes, God does make allowance for the carnal mind (Roms. 8:7) before he converts the mind (John 14:7). However, the step that follows must always be to go forward toward baptism so that a physical mind could be begotten and become one that is led by the Spirit even though that initial amount of the Spirit is extremely tiny leaving the new converted individuals still 99 percent carnal.

How would someone know they have been given, or grants (Acts 11:18; II Tim.2:25), the gift of repentance? Just as quickly as they have been really convicted concerning the depth of their sins in the past, then they have arrived at repentance. Of course, they will have to know what they are repenting of. The two verses that follow the command to repent and be baptized, Acts 2:36-37, describe a listening audience who were moved, even amazed by the perfect words in his sermon. They had just been told that they had, "You have crucified Jesus Christ." It was a statement that was shocking and the Greek expression from which his term is translated is Katanussa and the definition is, "To pierce thoroughly, shake up violently, shake up violently or sting immediately!"

All these terms are more powerful than the one that the translator chose, and they signify individuals who were all torn apart concerning what they had done. These people were shocked and sobered that their sins had really played a direct role in crucifying Christ. (Recall that these disciples were not the (stake). This is why we ask the question, "What shall we do?"

Peter had an answer. His answer was to "change." If Peter was speaking on this day, he would without a doubt exercise this phrase (change) rather than the Old King James English word repent, which, as before described, has the exact definition.

Close to the end of the book of Job realize a profound need to repent of the self-righteous attitude. The Bible tells us that he "abhorred himself" and repented in the dust and ashes (42:6).

The Hebrew phrase is exercised here, maac, meaning "spun, abhor, cast away, condemn, despise, disdain, loathe, refuse, reject, reprobate, utterly vile." These words make a strong phase picture of how the soon-to-be Christian must feel after they have been given the gift of repentance. Together with Act 2:38, the image can be seen more clearly.

The phrase "converts" means to extract something means to turn from. A Christian is one who turns from change from a way of life of sin to the way of God's righteousness through the power of God's Holy Spirit. The mind that repents is ready to do this for the time they have remaining on this Earth.

In addition to being able to come to repentance, individuals seeking baptism must ask themselves some important questions.

Did you completely prove that God does exist? When you hope, feel, believe, or think that He exists, it is not the same as proving He does exist? You must set out to prove this for yourself. You must know without a shadow of a doubt that God exists!

Did you find proof in the Scriptures that the Bible was inspired by God? Can you believe that the Bible is His Road Map that He put here on this earth for man to follow? Did you find proof that there is authority behind the Word of God? Have you made your mind up to be determined to not to live by bread alone, but every word that comes out of the mouth of God (Luke 4:4)?

Did you find proof that He is the real Church? There are well over 2,000 different denominations that are in the United States alone. While some people will say to you, the truth is, "They cannot all be wrong, the truth is they cannot all be right either." It was demonstrated that Christ built His Church, and it is not divided (Matt. 12:25; I Cor.10:13). You were able to see that it stands on the truth (I Tim. 3:15; John 8:31-32). It does not sleep in the same bed as iniquity (Gens. 2:17). Christ, not men, rules His Church. Did you, with satisfaction, find proof to yourself where God's Church is?

Christ talked about "counting up the cost" of becoming His

disciples (Luke 14:25-30). You will consider the cost if you purchase a car, a house, or a boat. Many people buy stuff they are not prepared for. They do not accurately plan for the unexpected hardships that could create a problem to make their day-to-day responsibility more challenging. Due to inaccurate financial planning, they cause their homes to be foreclosed and cars to be repossessed.

True Christianity works in the exact same manner. God placed an offer for your salvation so splendidly and magnificent to disobey illustration. But this does not come without a cost to you. Your friends and family might look at you in a different light-shun you even. The most precious traditions must be left behind. You might even be misunderstood or must endure persecution. Are you willing to trust Christ completely and if you must, will you leave your employment to follow Him? Are you prepared to put God first in your life no matter the cost?

So many questions: how can a person know for sure that God is calling? To get a call from God means that you can see, hear, and read the truth and understand it. God is giving you and exposing to you knowledge that you did not have before. James 4:17 tells us, "Therefore to him that knows to do good, and does it not, to him it is sin." This matter becomes extremely serious because Hebrews 10:26 tells us, "For if we sin willfully after that we have received the knowledge of the truth, there remains no more sacrifice for sins."

If you are getting the call from God, you really do not have any choice but to answer all these questions above with a yes.

When an individual has gone through the proper channels for counseling to fully understand the rules of repentance explained in this book, they are ready to be baptized. That person should then go ahead and get baptized just as quickly as a true servant of God becomes available to perform the baptism.

CHAPTER 8

BAPTISMAL SYMBOLS

There are many leading symbols that are used to represent baptism. Some of these symbols play an important role throughout the practice of baptism. They are water, the cross, a white garment, a font, oil, a candle, a dove, a flame, a seashell, chi-rho, and fish.

1. WATER BAPTISM

Water baptism is one of the key symbols of baptism. It is the Christian symbol of <u>divine life</u>; it is also a sign of purity and cleansing from sin. The outward sign of baptism is the actual pouring of the water on the head as these words are being recited. These are the words, "I baptize thee in the name of the Father, the Son, and the Holy Spirit." The cleansing quality of water is thought to be something that can purify an individual from the outside. The holy waters mean that life is given to humans by God and is a symbol of his grace. As well, water recalls the gospel, John 3:1-6, ".... unless a man is born of water and of Spirit, he cannot enter the kingdom of God..."

Water was used by John the Baptist (Jn. 3: 11; Mark 1: 8a; John 1: 33; 3: 23), as well as Jesus (Jn 3: 22). Jesus is the living water (Jn. 4: 10), and when Christ it was water flowing from his side assist was pierced, serving as a well of spring of Christ's life and grace (Jn 19: 34). The standard way is infusion, for water to be poured over the head. Baptism can also be done by a partial or full immersion. Water symbolizes divine life, grace, new birth, growth, deliverance, cleansing, and the covenant.

2. The Cross

The Cross is a symbol that is always present. It is used during baptism. The cross is a worldwide of Christianity. Creating a sign of the cross over the individual who is being baptized, especially children, while the baptism is taking place invokes the protection of God and asks for a child to enter the congregation of the Christian church. The symbol of the cross can be found in many Christian practices as well as in the Christian churches. As well the cross is a symbol of the crucifixion of Jesus. Jesus' death was his sacrifice to wash away all of humans' sins. The cross is one of the well-known symbols of the Christian Faith.

Once Christians make a motion to draw a cross, they renew the baptismal promises. The promises to deny Satan and all unholy forces.

3. Baptismal Garment

The baptismal garment is a type of clothing that is worn by people who get baptized. The clothing bears a reflection of a person being newly baptized and this person will become a new person in Christ, has been freed from all sins and is ready to accept God. White is also a color of purity and whenever someone wears a white garment during their baptism, it symbolizes that those people who are being baptized have a slate that has been wiped clean in God's eyes. It is the Christian's belief that every person is born with the "original sin," which can only be washed away through baptism. The white garment that the person wears symbolizes that the person is now clothed in the mantle of God and will begin a new and clean life in the Church's eyes.

4. Baptism Font

Traditionally, the Baptism Font is the basin that holds water that is used for the baptism. The Baptism Font symbolizes the baptism, streams, rivers, or pools of water in the past centuries, such as the Jordan River, where Christ was baptized by John the Baptist. In accordance with the tradition of specific denominations, a child is either immersed or dipped into the water.

Font or water from the Font is sprinkled or poured over a baby's head. Baptismal Fonts are made of stone, wood, metal, or marble and have normally been presented in the church for many years.

Baptism Font can be large pools in which an individual can be completely dipped, or they can be smaller fonts that the ministers use to sprinkle or pour baptismal the Holy Trinity—the Father, the Son, and the Holy Spirit.

In years past, the baptismal fonts were put in a separate room away from the congregation. However, currently, these fonts are frequently put at the entrance to the church or inside a noticeable location for much better or simpler access.

5. The Oil

Another baptismal symbol of the Holy Spirit is oil. The oil has two types. The Oil of the Catechumens is used after prayer of exorcism and the chest is anointed with it. In addition, it represents the Holy Spirit during sacraments and religious gatherings. Oil has been mentioned in the Bible a few times as a symbol of bringing people and the Holy Spirit together. Holy oils are used during baptism to strengthen an individual's faith. Additionally, they symbolize the gifts of the Holy Spirit. Oil also symbolizes salvation. Oil also represents salvation as well as the strength and power that comes from Christ our Savior. When a baby is baptized, it is anointed with oil. Oil strengthens the outcome of the anointed to change their minds about evil and temptation and sin, power that comes only from our Savior Jesus Christ. Following the pouring, sacred Chrism is used to anoint the crown of the head and it represents salvation, participation of the priesthood of Christ, membership in the congregation of Christ, and sharing of eternal life.

6. Baptismal Light (Candle)

Light symbolizes the baptism is represented by the passing of the lighted candle from the merrymaker to the godparents. The candle symbolizes a move from death to life in Christ. Light, as water, is important to the survival of life for the reason that without the light of the sun, nothing would be able to exist on this earth. Additionally, it is a symbol of genesis and is the vitality of life itself. The candle is also a symbol of Christ as the "Light of the world" and the Christian faith. When the candle is burning religious faith is present."

The candle is also lit from the Easter Candle. It is a representation of the risen Jesus, who is as mentioned above, the light of the world (Jn 8:12). Jesus is the light that leads everyone who has been baptized. It is also the flame that keeps faith burning so brightly.

7. The Dove

The dove, in Christianity, represents the symbolism of the Holy Spirit in baptism. In accordance with the Bible, the heavens opened up when Christ was baptized. The Holy Spirit descended upon Jesus in the shape of a dove during his water baptism and God spoke from heaven.

"And the Holy Ghost descended in a bodily shape like a dove upon him, and a voice from heaven, which said, thou art my beloved Son, in thee I am well pleased" (Luke 3:22).

Everyone who is baptized receives this same Holy Spirit. When a person is baptized, Jesus does so with the Holy Spirit (Mark 1:8; Jn 1:33).

The dove also confirmed that Jesus is God's Son. This

miraculous event shows the loving union between elements of the Christian Trinity: God the Father and man. When the dove came as a dove at the baptism of Jesus, it demonstrated that God (through the Son) would ultimately lead to reconciliation with God.

8. The Flame

The flame is generally affiliated with the Holy Spirit descending from the heavens as the tongues of fire during Pentecost. While water symbolizes purity and cleansing of the spirit, the flame symbolizes the Holy Spirit's transformation into the individual that is baptized.

9. The Seashell

Seashells were affiliated with baptism because they, on occasion, used the seashell to baptize his converts in Spain. The story went like this. St. James did not have anything else. Seashells also are symbols of the Virgin Mary. In certain stories, seashells are described as using only three drops of water, which is an indication of the Father, the Son, and the Holy Spirit.

10. The Chi-Rho

The Chi-Rho is one of the ancient Christian symbols and is frequently printed on objects that are affiliated with and used during the baptism. In Greek, the letters chi is affiliated with the English letter CH, and Rho is equal to the letter R. Once put together, the initial two letters of the Greek word for Christ. The symbols are used to represent Christ.

Chi-rho is printed on baptismal elements used during baptism to symbolize an individual is

baptized in the name of Jesus.

11. THE FISH

The Fish is among the ancient Christian symbols, partially arising from the perspective that Jesus was a fisher of men. It symbolizes the holy miracles that Jesus performed by multiplying the bread and a fish to feed the multitude. It also symbolizes the first meal that Christ had after his resurrection. The fish symbol is in addition, known as the Ichthys and was used during the time when Romans persecuted the Christians as a way to single out fellow Christians.

It is frequently believed that a fish represents the person who is baptized. In comparison, a set of fish represents the whole Christian community, keeping them all together in a net that protects them all. This net is known as the Christian church. Lastly, the fish represents the new life that an individual is given when an individual receives the baptism of the Holy Ghost. Once they are put in order, the three fishes represent and symbolize the Father, the Son, and the Holy Spirit.

CHAPTER 9

HOW TO LIVE FOR GOD NOT YOUR FEELINGS?

People live according to the way they feel more than anything else most of the time. If you stop long enough and listen, you will hear people as they speak concerning how they are feeling more than anything else. Do you often wonder whether we are serving the god of our emotions more than the God in the Word?

For instance, there are a few people who would say, I do not feel like God loves me. Let me tell you, God loves you when you do not love yourself. Get out of your feelings because God does not work with feelings. The Word of God tells us that God loves us and that he has a plan for us. But when we choose to believe the lies that our enemy places in our minds as opposed to believing what the Bible says, we get all up into our feelings and feel that our enemy is right then we live that lie.

Red Alert— Living by our Emotions is a Hazard

People who live by their emotions make huge errors when they make decisions based on how they feel instead of obeying the Heavenly Father and doing what they know in their hearts is the right thing to do.

We find in the Word that we do not wrestle against flesh and blood.

The Word frequently illustrates that the Christian life is a war against iniquity and the devil. The Christians are the soldiers of Christ in spiritual warfare (2 Corinthians 10:3, 4; 2 Timothy 2:3,4). When we read the Scripture, we find, "We do not wrestle against flesh and blood, but against.... spiritual hosts of wickedness," (Ephesians 6:12). "That is the purpose for Paul urging Christians to put on the whole armor of God, that you may be able to stand the wiles of the devil" (verse 11).

We will now examine each spiritual armor and understand how it can assist us in being victorious in the army for Christ in our war against the spiritual hosts of iniquity.

1. Belt of truth (Ephesians 6:14)

"Stand therefore, having girded your waist with the truth," Paul says. Truth is the belt that keeps all the other pieces of the armor in place. The truth holds up in two ways in the armor of God.

First, it represents the truths of the Word of God instead of the lies of Satan. Satan is the father of lies (John 8:44). Jesus said, "You shall know the truth, and the truth should make you free" (verse 32). The unlimited truth of the Word—the love of God, salvation through faith in Jesus Christ, the Second Coming, the forgiveness of sin, grace, and authority to live for Jesus—these truths sets us free from the lies of Satan. Satan makes us believe that we are filled with sin, have no hope, and that we are lost forever. The truth is that we have been set free, with no more shackles on our feet because of the love of God and His salvation. No more death.

Second, the truth serves as a belt, holding in place the full armor of God, which is our individual vow to uphold the truth—to dedicate our lives to a life of righteousness, visible, and without any deception. It is of the utmost importance that all not just some Christians walk in honesty and with integrity.'

The people should know that they can be able to depend upon you as a Christian, a soldier of truth and value.

2. Breastplate of righteousness

The breastplate of righteousness covers the heart and other critical organs. The Word tells us to "Keep your heart with all diligence, for out of it spring the issue of life" (Proverbs 4:25). That is what the goodness of Christ does for you. It safeguards you against each one of Satan's claims and allegations. Christ's goodness does not have anything to do with any good deeds you may or may not have done. God's Word made that clear when it was written in Romans 3:10, none of us are righteous in ourselves.

People often ask me how I feel. I responded by saying I am a blessed woman who is blessed by God and can't be cursed. I tell them I do not, and I cannot live by my feelings. I did not get out of my bed by myself when morning came. We must learn to live past our emotions, even when we are wrong.

People ask me on a constant basis how I feel concerning different things. How do you feel about traveling, for example? I answer them by saying that I have learned over the years not to live by my feelings. There is that big chance that I will not do what I know is right in the sight of God. I travel, but not so much. My feelings are that I would rather be home resting. I feel like the hotel is too expensive and staying with your relatives—well, I'd rather not get into that one.

The breastplate of righteousness is the complete righteousness of Christ, which he freely gives us after we embrace him as our Savior (Corinthians 5:21; Ephesians 2:8, 9; Philippians 3:9). It is Jesus's righteousness—not our personal righteousness—that shields and keeps us safe from the wickedness of Satan.

3. Shoes of the gospel (Ephesians 6:15)

As the soldiers marched into battle, their feet must be fitted with shoes that are comfortable. Being soldiers of Christ's army, we must put on gospel shoes that will permit us to march wherever Christ leads. The apostle John says, "He who says he abides in Him [Jesus] ought himself also to walk just as He [Jesus] walked" (1 John 2:6). Jesus said, "My sheep hear My voice, . . . and they follow Me" (John 10:27). Satan will continuously attempt to put barriers in our path; however, we will always have the strength of Jesus so that we will be able to continue our forward march, following our Savior, obeying him, and climbing to higher heights in the gospel.

4. Shield of Faith (Ephesians 6:16)

Reading about the different parts of the armor of God, Paul says, "Above all, . . . [Take] the shield of faith with which you will be able to quench all the fiery darts of the wicked one," (Ephesians 6:16).

When Satan attacks with doubts, the shield of faith turns aside the blow. When temptations come, faith keeps us steadfast in following Jesus. We can withstand all the devil's fiery darts because we know whom we have believed (2 Timothy 3:12).

This is not a faith that comes from inside us. This faith is much bigger than that, it is a gift that God has given us. He gives each of us a measure of faith (Romans 12:3). Afterwards, we walk with him, increase, and expand until it turns into a shield, which guards us and permits us to a life of victory in Christ Jesus. This is what Paul got a taste of. He said, "I have been crucified with Christ; it is no longer I who live, but Christ lives in me; and the life which I now live in the flesh I live by faith in the Son of God, who loved me and gave himself for me," (Galatians 2:20). And at the completion of that life of faith, he proclaimed, "I have fought the good fight, I have finished the race, I have kept the faith," (2 Timothy 4:7). You can also get a taste of this life, as you tap into this shield of faith to escape from Satan.

I decided a long time ago to follow God's will and the plan he has for me because I found out that feelings will get you in a lot of trouble. Trouble sometimes that only God can get you out of. I learned to lean on the Bible and let it order my steps in the LORD. In doing this, I cannot go wrong. I have made up my mind that I want to be a blessing to others and make decisions that are pleasing to God.

5. Helmet of salvation (Ephesians 6:17)

Like the helmet for a bike or a motorbike, it protects the head. It is probably the most crucial part of the body because it is the engine that controls your thoughts and the mind. We can get a thorough understanding of our salvation; Satan will not make us move by his trickery. The moment we realize that we are journeying on with Christ and our sins are forgiven, we will have a peace that cannot be disrupted in any way by Satan.

Can we be guaranteed salvation? Can we have assurance?

Yes, "If we confess our sins, he [Jesus] is faithful and just to forgive us our sins and to cleanse us from all unrighteousness," (1 John 1:9). "God has given us eternal life, and this life is in His Son. He who has the Son has life," (1 John 5:11, 12).

6. Sword of the Spirit (Ephesians 6:17)

The sword of the spirit is a weapon and the only weapon listed in the armor of God. Every other protective defense is in nature. The Word of God is portrayed as the "living and powerful, and sharper than any two-edged sword," (Hebrews 4:12). This weapon was used by Christ in the wilderness when Satan tempted him. With every attempt that Satan used to lead him into sin, Christ answered, "It is written. . . ," (John 17:17). That is the reason it is so mighty. It is also the reason it is so vital that we study the Word and get acquainted with its truth and its strength. David wrote, "Your word is a lamp unto my feet and a light to my path," (Psalm 119:105). The sword is the Word of God, both saves us from harm and defeats our adversary—Satan and his temptations.

7. Prayer (Ephesians 6:18)

Even though prayer is not one of the parts of the whole armor of God, still Paul concludes his list with these words, "Praying always with all prayer and supplication in the Spirit," (Ephesians 6:18). Just as you are fully dressed in the whole armor of God, it is essential to immerse it all in prayer. When you pray, it brings you into communion and fellowship with our Heavenly Father so that his armor can shield the enemy.

8. How do you put on the whole armor of God?

It is not as challenging as one may believe. Every part of the armor will be discovered as your relationship with Christ grows. This is the way Paul said it, "Put on the Lord Jesus Christ," (Romans

13:14). When you willingly give your life to Christ and put on "His righteousness, you are dressed in the whole armor of God.

Do you feel weak on occasion? Do you notice that you give into temptation when you desire to triumph over the enemy? Do not become discouraged. Everyone experiences these moments. However, dressed in the whole armor of God, the weakest of his children is greater than a match for the devil. In Christ, dressed in the Heavenly Father's unconquerable armor, you will, "Be strong in the Lord and in the power of His might." You will "Be able to stand against the wiles of the devil," (Ephesians 6:10, 11).

Breathing is a must for us to grow.

Spiritually, we must breathe. Our prayers become the breath of our fibers. I Thessalonians 5:17 tells us to "pray continually." And in Romans 2:12 we read, "faithful in prayer." "Do not be anxious about anything, but in everything, by prayer and petition, with thanksgiving, present your requests to God," (Philippians 4:6).

Prayer is the key that opens our souls to our Heavenly Father as we do to a friend, "Ask, and it will be given to you," (Matthew 7:7). When we pray to God, His answer has such a great melody and a more pleasing experience. It is the very breath of our essence. If we do not have a prayer life, then the spiritual man will quickly deteriorate from lack of any other necessities. (See Matthew 7:7 and Mark 11:24).

When we exercise, we grow.

The third thing we must do is exercise or get involved in Christian work. God has a vineyard, and we must work in it. (Matthew 21:28) Which part should we work in? If you will read Mark 16:15, you will find that it says,"Go into all the world and preach the good news to all creation." Jesus came into the world, "... not to be served, but to serve, and to give His life as a ransom for many," (Matthew 20:28).

CHAPTER 10

WHAT DETERMINES THE WAY YOU LIVE?

As we grow closer to God, we get wiser and learn how to get over our feelings and do that which is right in the sight of the LORD, even when we feel wrong. I mean, how many times have you said, "I feel like... "or " don't feel like...." And then what do you feel? Do you allow your feelings to determine how you treat others? Or what do you say? Do you allow your emotions to run your life? But somehow, in the end, I would always trust God and allow Him to let the Holy Spirit step in and everything seems to maliciously work out. I let my feelings of insecurity go and put my confidence in God. There were so many times I felt so angry with my husband and I felt like turning my back to him and not speak to him and not cook for a day or two, but I would decide to pray instead and ask God for His grace, so I can have a heart to forgive him or ask him for his forgiveness, that gives me the ability to treat him the way God will have me to treat him.

The key is not allowing us to be so quick to react but making a conscious decision to do that which is right in the sight of God. I am not saying that this is always easy, but to live for God you must do this. You just must always remember that it is not always about how you feel because it is not about you, not even me, it is about God.

How to Live for God

Have you accepted Jesus Christ as your Lord and Savior? Have your sins been forgiven (Rom 8:16)? Have you been born again, and do you truly desire to live for Go? If so, there are five things you must be sure of:

First, be sure of your own salvation.

You need to know in your heart that you are saved. How can you know that you are saved? The answer is the Word of God. When you are washed in the blood of Jesus, that gives you safety from the enemy, and the Word of God makes you sure. These things have I written unto you... that ye may **know** that you have eternal life (1 John 5:13).

"Him that cometh to me I will in no wise cast out," (John 6: 37). Have you gone to Him with a willing heart and a made-up mind? Are you in or out? God said he would not cast you out. Then he must take you in. You see, it is not about your feelings. It all hinges on the Word of God. Having faith in what the Heavenly Father says.

Second, do not be afraid to show a man that you stand for Christ.

Do not be one who believes only in secret, it will not work. Openly confess every chance you get. Jesus said in the Word that if you are ashamed to own Him before man, that he will deny you before His Father. "Whosoever therefore shall be ashamed of me and of my words... of him also shall the Son of man be ashamed," (Mark 8: 38). If you desire to have fast growth in the Lord, you must confess Him openly.

Third, turn away from **all** your wrongdoings.

God wipes your slate clean. You get a fresh start. God provides you with a new nature, one that causes you to love righteousness and hate sins. You are now able to overcome the world. Sin has no more power over you. God said it in the Bible, "Sin shall not have dominion over you" (Rom. 6: 14). However, you must choose righteousness and forsake your sinful ways. Turn your back on sin, now. Put it behind you and do not look back. "Let not sin therefore reign in your mortal body," (Rom. 6: 12). Clean yourself up from sin and be finished with it once and for all.

Fourth, give yourself more time for Bible study and prayer.

The more you read the Bible, the more you will find that you want to spend time reading it. If you have a desire to grow in grace, have a meeting with the Father daily. Find a place where you and God can have that time for prayer and Bible study. You do not want any disturbance. Just you and God. You want to be a Bible Christian. Do not ever let a day go by without spending time alone with the Heavenly. "As newborn babes, desire the sincere milk of the word, that ye may grow thereby," (1 Peter 2:2).

Fifth, Keep yourself busy in the service of Heavenly Father.

Satan will continuously find a way to be mischievous in the presence of idle hands. Therefore, do not sit around doing nothing. Put yourself to work. Find something to do. Get yourself into a church that is strictly for winning souls for the LORD. Join the choir. Join the Pastor's Aid Club. Help with the work of the youth. Make yourself available for prayer meetings. Put your priorities in perspective. Know that God always comes first. Get in a church where God is present, the people are being converted and where the true message is going forth, "Ye must be born again." If you can follow these easy steps, you will be a positive and cheerful Christian. God will be able to use you in His service, and you will find that you will be a blessing wherever you choose to go.

CHAPTER 11

WHAT MUST I DO TO PLEASE GOD, AND WHAT IS IT TO CONSIST OF TO BE A TRUE CHRISTIAN?

"Not everyone who says to me, Lord, Lord, will enter the kingdom of heaven," said Jesus. But the one that is doing the will of the Father will enter the kingdom of heaven (Mt. 7: 21). Confessing to Christianity does not please God by confessing it, but by putting it into action. The true followers of Christ consist of their total walk of life, take accountability of their way of behaving toward money, nonspiritual labor, performing, experienced traditions, and commemorations, their attitudes toward their husbands and wives, and other interactions with humanity. Christians who are not true, on the other hand, accept the belief and the ways of the world, which has grown to be more and more sinful throughout these final days (Ps.92: 7).

How can we put God's word into Action, as found in Malachi 3:18 in our Life?

In accordance with the prophet Malachi, "You people will again certainly see the distinction between a righteous one and a wicked one, between one serving God and one who has not served him." (Mal. 3:18) As you look back on those writings, question yourself, Do I mix with this world, or do I stick out like a sore thumb? Am I forever trying to cope with the crowd at school and at my place of work, or do I stand unmoved on the beliefs of the Bible; when it is applicable, do I speak up? (Read I Peter 3:16)

Naturally, we do not aspire to give the impression that we are self-righteous. However, we must stick out as distinctive from the people who do not show their love for or serve God.

If you reflect on it and find that it is an opportunity for change for the better, why shouldn't you consult with God about the situation and search out a heavenly power by way of prayer, Bible study, and conference appearance. "The more God Word becomes a part of you, the more you will produce fine fruit, including the fruit of lips which make public declarations to God's name," (Heb.13: 15).

What must One do to become a True Christian?

For a person to become a true Christian, he or she must confess their sins and be baptized. To be baptized, one must be fully immersed in the water, the name of Jesus. The reason for being in the water is your old man must die to sin and a new man must arise. Well, what do I mean a new man must arise? Your life should change. It is a process.

Challenges of the Christian might not be the same. However, most of the Christians are caught up in the chief conflicts of their mind. II Corinthians 5:17 might seem as if it is magnificent, "Therefore, if anyone is in Christ, he is a new creation; the old has gone, the new has come!" (NIV). However, when the truth sets it —we will all fall short of the glory of God, particularly with our thought process.

Our old way of thinking has been terminated, but most of us continue to struggle with temptations that are yet lingering in our minds. We still struggle with the evils of animosity, downheartedness, anxiety, fruitlessness, irritations, and difficulties.

The meaning of an effective Christian is to follow Jesus, to be obedient to His teaching, to love one another and to be at a place where you can spiritually grow. This does not stop the struggles that are ranting and raving in our minds.

The LORD has an answer to this struggle, and it is not as

simple as praying. It is crucial to pray. However, more is demanded than just prayer. Romans 12:2 gets right to the core of the issue and God also provides an answer, "Do not conform any longer to the pattern of this world but be transformed by the renewing of your mind. Then you will be able to test and approve what God's will is his good, pleasing, and perfect will." (NIV)

The vow is strong if you renew your mind. The LORD has even thrown in one or two remarkable benefits and bonuses.

1. You will be changed. Not only will you be cleansed from the outside, but you will have a total change on the inside as well.
2. You will realize and have a knowledge of God's will for your life.
3. How many times have you told yourself, "I wish I knew what God wanted me to do in this situation?" You now have a road map to the will of the LORD. "His great, gratifying, and flawless will. Renew your mind!"
4. He is the God of peace, and He will be with you when you renew your mind. Read Philippians 4:8-9.

And be renewed in the spirit of your mind, "And that you put away the old man and put on the new man after God has created righteousness and true holiness. Wherefore put away lying and SPEAK EVERY NATURAL TRUTH WITH HIS NEIGHBOR, for we are members one of another," (Ephes. 4: 23, 24).

Read also Romans 12:2, Philippians 4:8,9, and Hebrews 3:1. These three scriptures tell you that you must renew your mind. You will not find any scriptures that say if you pray, God will renew your mind. As far as renewing your mind, God will do his part, you just need to do your part.

The Holy Spirit will guide you into all truth (John 16:13).

When you become saved, you are no longer your old self. The Word of God says, "Behold, all things are new, and the old things are done away with." The way you used to think can no longer be. As I have said above, it is a process, not a one-time accomplishment. To enable yourself to do this, you should pray a sincere prayer. With this sincere prayer you can also add 8 specific steps that are found in Philippians 4:8, 9.

"Finally, brothers, whatever is true, whatever is noble, whatever is right, whatever is pure, whatever is lovely, whatever is admirable if anything is excellent or praiseworthy-think about such things. Whatever you have learned or received or heard from me or seen in me, put it into practice. And the God of peace will be with you," Philippians 4:8-9 (NIV).

By using each of these 8 steps, my mind can be sifted to come nearer to God's way of thinking. Working with these 8 steps, I must continually seek out God's requirement, not mine. For instance, I must think about which is true. I need to find out what is the truth of God and not what my opinion of the truth is. It is not about me, nor is it about you. It is about Jesus Christ.

What is it that God says concerning His truth? This is what I must fill my mind with. For me to be able to do this, I must read the Word of God each day. I need to be able to memorize the Word. This is the only way. By the renewing of my mind, I will be inclined to change my way of deeds. I cannot just read the information and sit on it. I must act on it as well. Do not just read the 8 steps. I challenge you to put them into action and see how your life will drastically transform by the renewing of your mind. God will do the rest.

Put down your train of thought and let God's thoughts come into your mind. God said in His Word that your thoughts are not my thoughts, and neither are your ways my ways (Isaiah 55:8), (KJV).

As I mentioned above, this is a process, if you feel in any way that you have fallen short of one or more of these 8 steps, don't beat yourself up about it. Just get back up, brush yourself off, and get back to each of the 8 steps. You did not become a sinner overnight, so you are not going to become a Christian overnight. After all, as the old saying goes, "Rome was not built overnight."

With the usage of each of the 8 steps in Philippians 4:8, you can get the assistance you need to renew your mind. Fill your mind with God's Word that connects to that step. If you begin to have any challenges with any of those areas, then write them down and start to speak to those problems with authority. Carry them on your personal and read them all through your day. Filling your mind with His truth throughout the day will benefit you and the more you do it the better. This will aid you in cleansing your mind of all unacceptable thoughts.

The bottom line here is, what kind of thoughts do you want to have in your mind? To learn to think like Christ involves you constantly making decisions in your mind. It is your mind and your decision alone. God will not force himself on you. You will have to want it, and the decision must be all on your own for you to transform.

In the Old Testament, Joseph was sold into slavery by his brothers. As a slave, his journey took him into Egypt and ultimately, he was thrown into prison for a deed he did not do. He had lost all hope for a future. God rescued him. You will not read anywhere in the scriptures that Joseph turned bitter because of this unfairness that agonized his life.

Several eons afterward, his brothers thought that he was going to take revenge for the wrongful act they did to him, but he didn't. What Joseph demonstrated was truly remarkable. He showed a renewing of the mind. "While you brothers did it to harm me, God meant it for my good. He did it to achieve what was to take place in the future. God allowed it so that Joseph would be able to save the many lives that would be impacted by famine. Now, then, rid yourself of any fear you may have. God said in His Word that he would be a provider for you and your children. He restored their confidence and most of all he had only kind words for them," (Genesis. 50:20-21).

We Develop by Eating

First, we must eat. What is the right food for our spiritual lives? "The words I have spoken to you are spirit and they are life," (John 6:63). "When your words came, I ate them: they were my joy and my heart's delight," (Jeremiah 15:16). Reading and studying the Bible daily is a must for spiritual growth and the very essence of life. Our souls will not survive if we do not eat this food; we will not develop as we should and ultimately waste away spiritually.

We must put on the whole armor of God to have that spiritual walk with God. What is the Armor of God? The armor of God, you will find in Ephesians 6:10-18, consists of the following items: the belt of truth, the breastplate of righteousness, the shoes of the gospel, the shield of faith, the helmet of salvation, and the sword of the spirit. A list and description of the full armor of God can be found below.

Been Chosen

"For many are called, but a few are **chosen.**" (Matthew 22:14). The Word of God tells us that many people are called to be members of the Heavenly ministry. However, sadly, not everyone is chosen. God only selects a few people who are chosen to become a priest after being called.

"Yet you have a few people in Sardis who have not soiled their clothes. They will walk with me, dress in white, for they are worthy," (Revelation 3:4).

The puzzle here to be resolved is after we have been called to the ministry, then what? How do we become one of the chosen few? The answer to this puzzle is that we must demonstrate that we are worthy of such a high honor.

"Anyone who loves his father or mother more than me is not worthy of me; anyone who loves his son or daughter more is not worthy of me; and anyone who does not pick up his cross and follow me is not worthy of me," (Mathew 10:37, 38).

There is not much preaching on the subject concerning the necessity for the people to be worthy of Christ and the Kingdom of God. What is the reason behind this? It is my belief that people are terrified of speaking that will scare the people, so they only give out a portion of the Word instead. Perhaps the people will walk away and not receive the Gospel of Christ and not get saved.

Consequently, Christians, at least in America, do not really know the severity of how firm the demands of Christ truly are. Therefore, people who attend church might not be as seasoned as Christ would yearn for them to be. There is not any hesitation that the righteous discernment that is on the vanishing point for America will be the reason for a whole lot of people who are not fully developed to come to Christ, something that was not done previously. By doing this, they will cause the people to become a chosen person.

As a prisoner for the Lord, I urge you to live a life worthy of the calling you have received (Ephesians 4: 1).

Jesus is worthy of praise is a true statement. The same holds that the life we live is worthy of our calling as ministers of God. This way, we leave from the positions of being called into to being put in the position to be chosen.

No matter what transpires, carry yourself in a way that is deserving of the praise of the Gospel of Christ. Then, whether I come and see or only hear about you in absence, I will know you stood firm in one spirit, contending as one man in the faith of the gospel. (Philippians 1: 27)

We were called. We were pedestrians to be chosen.

Encouraging, comforting, and urging you to live of God, who calls you into his kingdom and glory. (I Thessalonians 2:12)

As a result, we do realize that there is more to being a Christian than simply agreeing to receive Christ for one reason and then returning to the previous state of how you lived. To be found worthy of Christ and His kingdom, you must fully dedicate your whole life to the Lord. You must give up your worldly life and clean yourselves up from a sinful life. To do this, you must be led by the spirit of God, and you must continue washing your robe in the blood of the Lamb.

In the United States, it is very smart to abruptly sense the need to repent. A revival is held where many people attend, and a lot of individuals repent and ask the LORD God to heal the land.

This is better than coming up empty-handed. However, this is not the way a Christian becomes worthy of the Kingdom. A

Christian must constantly walk in the acknowledgment of their sins and atonement. This is what is meant by washing our robe in the blood of the Lamb. You cannot do this by going to a citywide festivity of Godly remorse, in which individuals shed a bunch of tears over the ethical condition of their country and go back home and live the same way as before. One problem with that is since preachers are not preaching and teaching God's laws of grace. Individuals do not see the way of their errors, therefore, do not see where they need repentance. If we see ourselves perfect in Christ, and God sees us through Christ, we Christians do not see a need to repent.

Nothing in all creation is hidden from God's sight. Everything is uncovered and laid bare before the eyes of him to whom we must give account. (Hebrews 4:13)

We will not ever leave the level of being called and pass through to the level of being chosen until we demonstrate our deeds of being worthy of Christ and His Kingdom.

They will make war against the Lamb, but the Lamb will overcome them because he is Lord of lords and King of kings and with him will be his called, **chosen,** and faithful followers. (Revelation 17:14)

God has made vows to the people who follow Him, they will have an everlasting life with Jesus Christ. This is an occasion that is higher than any other.

Nevertheless, when we think about Revelation 17: 14 (above), we understand that to live eternally with Jesus, we must not simply be called and chosen but faithful as well.

To say yes to our calling, our provocation, to belong to Jesus, generally is not very hard. It will be necessary for you to humble yourselves, but for the most part, it is an easy thing to do. In some instances, I understand that in a nation that is overrun by the Muslim religion, to take the first step toward becoming a Christian, an individual or their family members might be persecuted, brutalized, or even put to death.

To go from being called to being chosen, you must deny yourself and take up the cross, and follow Jesus daily. For many people who are simply congregants, this is not the case. In America, they are simply churchgoers. It is my belief that this strong dedication is not the circumstance with a lot of worshippers. Thus, they are among many who have been called but not chosen.

Among those who have been called and chosen are proven to be faithful and acknowledge what is meant when I say it is very challenging to take a stand, demanding a great deal of patience, perseverance, and not be afraid. This clearly was the situation with the Apostle Paul. Paul sentenced himself to death so much that he could not trust himself, trusting only God, who raises the dead.

As warned by the Apostles, we must go through a lot of trials and tribulations to be able to endure them to be able to enter the Kingdom of Heaven.

Once we are chosen, we have a great deal to learn. We begin to hear voices in our minds, and have a lot of emotions that are not true. On occasions, it is nearly impractical to distinguish if the voice is from God or Satan. We wonder as to whether it is God or not. We might even give ourselves into inactiveness and wavering attempting to be a "hollow vessel."

Every type of dishonesty, ensnares, temptation, rests in our thoughts, untrue emotions of all types. Each of those who are guided by the Spirit are the sons of God. This is stated in the Bible. However, training to be guided by the Spirit would take a very long period as we stumble through the deceitful imitation forced on us by Satan's imps.

We probably might be suffering from some life-threatening ailment, and we pray, but we do not receive healing.

We automatically take it upon ourselves to blame the Lord for this sickness. We begin to believe that this is to make us remain defenseless and meek, but this certainly is not the case. We must not be so quick to blame the Lord unless He comes and tells us that this is what is taking place, the same as he did with Paul. It is probably well that if we should continue to praise the LORD for His greatness and ask for healing, he will heal us.

Just so you know, we never attempt to heal ourselves with some method we found in some book that is designed to explain the correlation between what we are diagnosed with and our mindset and conduct. When we begin to go through trials and tribulations, we should call on Jesus, making no effort to exercise our faith or another supernatural assumption.

When you are going through this, call upon Jesus. You do not understand anything. Place your hands in His nail-driven hands.

We have a lot to take in. God gives us revelations or dreams of what His plans are for us. It is between the years of the visions and the achievements that the holy people of God are shaped.

God is the translator of his own messages. If He gives you a message that you will dance with Him amid the stars, you must not presuppose that He means the stars who live in Hollywood. It just might be the stars in the heavens. Or it could be with the elementary students who receive stars for doing great in their class work. Let God do His own translations.

We must take one step at a time as we follow blindly to travel along our journey.

There will be occasions when we will feel as though The Heavenly Archer is preparing to lift His bow in the direction of their target; however, the bullseye will not be noticed for many years to come.

Many years can pass, we will not understand what it is that God is doing with us. We begin to make phony attempts, only to find out that we have moved too fast and have taken ourselves off the path that God had placed us on.

Until you have gone through the program of study that steers you in the direction of proving you are faithful, these words might mean a thing to you. However, once you start to remember, you will begin to recognize that they came to the exact tribulation that you are now having. God is completely faithful. If we are to be a representation of Him, we will have to be fully faithful. You cannot find a middle ground. If we are fans of blissfulness, it will be a challenge to continue to dance with the Fire of Israel. There should be sufficient press in our hearts that we do not give up no matter how long it takes us to be in captivity, no matter how long it takes until our greatest powerful yearnings are postponed.

If we plan to be with the Lord for all eternity, we will be able to be with Him everywhere He goes. We cannot have a lying tongue in our body. We cannot worship any idols. We must practice godliness and give up our confidentiality so He can be with us continuously.

Strong uprightness, powerful godliness, unyielding submission to God Almighty.

However, you are a chosen people, a royal priesthood, a holy nation, a people belonging to God, that you might declare the praises of him who called you out of the darkness into the wonderful light (I Peter 2:9).

Chapter 12

Who are God's True Followers?

The world has many thoughts on what it thinks concerning what a true Christian is or is not. You have some who believe that true Christians are naturally born into a family of Christians who admit to being Christians since they are blessed by a preacher. You have those who have this belief that a Christian is an individual who has completely given their heart and mind to God and is born again—or maybe a person who plainly professes that they are, in fact a Christian.

On the other hand, would it likely be viable for a person to live and die pretentiously thinking that they are a Christian—just to discover when they are judged by the Lord that they were never seen as a true Christian in the eyes of God? When reading, Matt. 7:21-23, we are warned by Jesus of this risk.

What will make an individual a true Christian? How does the LORD define a Christian in the Bible?

"Every good tree produces good fruit, but every rotten tree produces worthless fruit." Mat. 7: 17

How shall the true followers of Christ be separated from the false followers of Christ?

Jesus declared that the way to be able to tell the real followers is by the fruit that they produce. By the fruit-, I mean how they teach and their performance. (Mat. 7: 15-17, 20) People are affected by what they receive in their minds and hearts. (Mat. 15: 18,19) Those who allow their mind to be fed with carnal truths will produce fruit that is not good, but those who permit themselves to be taught spiritual truths will produce good fruit.

The two types of fruits have evidently turned out to be established throughout the end of time (Read Daniel 12: 3,10). Christians who are not true have an inaccurate interpretation of the LORD and frequently false structure of godly love, although those who have divine intuition reverence God in "spirit and in truth" (John 4: 24, 2 Tim. 3: 1-5). They do their best to exhibit behaviors that are Christlike. However, what about us individually? As you think about pursuing five distinguishing features of real Christianity, ask yourself: Is my behavior and beliefs distinctly coordinated with the Word of God? Am I improving the truth in the sight of those who seek for it?

Those followers who have a sincere heart about following Christ will wholeheartedly study their Bible so that they may be able to understand the real meaning of what a Christian is. They will also make sure that they are Christians who are really true to the Word of God (II Timothy 3: 15-17). Their hearts and minds will be set on loving both God and Jesus with all their heart and with all their mind and with all their strength (Mark 12: 28-30). They will dedicate themselves to living their lives by the one true Word of God (Matt. 4:4; Luke 4:4; Deut 8:3). They will be devoted to verifying everything from the Bible (I Thess. 5:21; Acts 17:10-12).

Eight Steps You Can Take to Renew Your Mind

Philippians 4:8-9 Strategy of Renewing Your Mind

1. Select one personality feature each day or each week. The initial one is genuine.

2. Continually tell yourself all through the day that you wish to do an individual examination on how great you are at employing this step to renew your mind.

Question yourself—what did I think about today? Was it true? Was it not true? Was I living out an imagination in my mind? Am I agonizing over what may occur? Is that the truth?

Am I taking a chance on the drive or thinking of another individual?

One method in assisting in assessing a thought is to question yourself if this was the Lord, what would be his thoughts concerning this problem or this individual?

3. Think about the reverse of that attribute. The reverse of genuine is dishonesty, imagination, and assumptions. Question yourself: Am I thinking concerning something that is untrue? If I am, then I need to quit heading down that pathway of thoughts.

4. What Bible verses will assist me in the application of this feature with my method of thinking?

What verses in the Bible on truth speak to you? Read the books of Proverbs and Psalms and you will find plenty of resources in the scriptures to exercise the 8 steps. Learn the scripture and think about it throughout each day's actions.

5. When you have gone through each of the 8 steps of Philippians 4:8, start to put into effect one of the challenges to every thought.

A youthful male will observe a beautiful, youthful female and think she is gorgeous. I would like to know what it would be like to be in a marital relationship with her.

His thought comes across the "whatever is true" test. However, if she is already the wife of someone else, this thought has failed the "whatever is true" test.

The procedure of renewing the mind demands us to take greater measures of cleaning our thoughts and assigning restrictions so that we will not head down a road of evil in our minds. Christ made it plain and simple in Matthew 5:27-28, that evil is not just evaluated by our deeds-we as well do evil when we adopt that thought and head down that road in our mind.

6. After you have assessed your thoughts, make sure you have the LORD in your psychological discussion. Say a prayer to the LORD first, ask Him to give you wisdom. Recite the Word as a prayer of what you desire God to do.

The prayer of David in Psalm 51:10 could be your prayer. "Create in me a pure heart, O God, and renew a steadfast spirit within me," (NIV).

7. Have a conversation with other Christians concerning the difficulties you are having in practicing these 8 steps to renewing your mind.

8. Whatever is excellent or praiseworthy?

Discuss your achievements and your difficulties. When you discuss with others, you open the door to strengthening new thought patterns. As well it can provide you with something optimistic to speak about.

It is now time to shift past the weather and sports of these discussions.

Do your emotions influence your thoughts?

Do you find it simpler to think optimistic thoughts after you have a sense that everything is going great? However, how do you answer when you are down in the dumps, demoralized, not interested, or saddened? Do you permit these emotions to manipulate your thoughts?

The LORD has made a vow to provide His children with the "spirit of self-discipline." Read II Timothy 1:7. If you have plans to renew your mind, self-discipline is a must.

The invitation to Christian wisdom is to control your thoughts and your feelings—to discover the equilibrium Christ had in three areas of His life- His thoughts, deeds, and emotions.

"Right thinking" leads to "right actions," which leads to" right feelings." The urgency is essential. If emotions are at the front, then they are in the driver's seat and they will propel you wherever they wish to carry you. There's an old saying, if it feels this good, then it must be the right thing to do. Do not do it. It is a trap! Your feelings will take you into every type of misperception.

"Right thinking" guides us in responding with "right actions." The correct emotions might not happen right away; however, they will get there in the end.

Say that you will take the test so that when you are feeling great, you should step back to third place in your priorities. The correct thinking is established upon observing every situation from the LORD's viewpoint and then the correct deeds-what would Christ do?

CHAPTER 13

WHO ARE THE CHRISTIANS?

To some, Christians are people who were born into a nation of Christians, or you come from a Christian background. Others think that you have a belief in Jesus or a religion based on the teachings of Jesus. Still, there are others who employ the phrase "Christian" to discuss a much more profound connection to Jesus Christ and an individual.

Because the Word of God has authority over the Christian faith, we will look and see what it says concerning the term "Christian." The term "Christian" is found in the New Testament only on three occasions and each time it is related to the first "Christian" in the early church.

"... So, for a whole year Barnabas and Saul met with the church and taught a great number of people. The disciples were called Christians first at Antioch," (Acts 11:26).

"Then Agrippa said to Paul, 'Do you think that in such a short time you can persuade me to be a Christian?' (Acts 26:28).

"However, if you suffer as a Christian, do not be ashamed, but praise God that you bear that name," (1 Peter 4:16).

They were called "Christians" because of how they conducted themselves, the things that they did, and because they acted in the same manner Christ did. The term "Christian" does mean followers of Christ or having its place in the gathering of Christ.

The question now is what made them a function of this assembly called "Christian?"

In the Word, you will find that it says that the good work that you do will not cause God to just take you into his warm, loving hands. This means that an individual can feed the poor, be in good standing with the community, attend church, and still serve their fellow citizens, but that will not make them a follower of Christ or a "Christian."

"At one time we too were foolish, disobedient, deceived, and enslaved by all kinds of passions and pleasures. We lived in malice and envy, being hated and hating one another. But when the kindness and the love of God our Savior appeared, **not because of righteous things we had done, but because of his mercy.** He saved us through the washing of rebirth and renewal by the Holy Spirit, whom he poured out on us generously through Jesus Christ our Savior, so that, having been justified by his grace, we might become heirs having the hope of eternal life," (Titus 3:3-6).

"For it is by grace you have been saved, through faith—and this is not from yourselves, it is the gift of God—not by works, so that no one can boast," (Ephesians 2:8-9).

The scripture above is openly shared with you that once we are born again or have salvation is really a gift from our Heavenly Father. In other words, you cannot earn salvation. When an individual accepts the real salvation from God, then and only then will they become a true "Christian" and place their faith in the hands of Christ. It also involves you accepting that Jesus died on the cross to pay for our sins and his rising from the grave again proves that he has power over death.

If you have not ever accepted the free gifts of God, I am encouraging you not to stop here. Continue this research with the gift of God. Is there anything holding you back? If it is, ask yourself if it is worth it. Do you still need some questions answered?

Have you made your mind up to trust Christ with all your **heart** to become a Christian and commit your life to Him? You need to know that your sins separate you from God (Romans 6:23), and Jesus died for you on the cross for your sins (Romans 5:8). If you will only have faith, Jesus can forgive you of your sins and he will give you life everlasting with him instead of you facing eternal damnation in hell.

Have a little conversation with God and let him know that you desire him to come into your life.

Note: Just because you pray a prayer, it does not mean that you are now saved. You are merely making known to God that you have faith in him through prayer.

"Father, I realize that I have failed to carry out the laws you have put before me. I also know that I have allowed my sins to separate me from you. I apologize for breaking your laws and now, I desire to turn away from my past sinful life that I have toward you. I am asking you to please forgive me. I believe that Jesus Christ is your Son and that he died on the cross for my sins. It is my belief, also that he rose from the dead, is very much alive, and that he hears my prayer. I invite Jesus into my life to become my Lord and Savior. He has now become my ruler and will as well reign in my heart from this day forward. Please send your Holy Spirit to help me to obey You, and to guide me as I embark upon this journey. To do Your will for the rest of my life. To obey You. In Jesus name, I pray. Amen"

"Repent and let every one of you be baptized in the name of Jesus Christ for the remission of sins; and you shall receive the gift of the Holy Spirit," (Acts 2:38).

Since you have studied all of this, have you planned to turn your life over to Christ today and welcome God into your family?

Scripture says if we will willingly make the following commitment.

- Obey Christ's commandment and be baptized.
- Let others know about your new faith in Christ.
- Do not let a day go by without spending time with God. You can ease into it within short periods of time. Make it a point to pray to God daily and read your Bible. If you do not understand the Word when you read it, pray and ask God for understanding and to deepen your knowledge of his Word.
- Pursue the spiritual union with others who are followers of Christ. Get yourself in the company of other believers to answer any questions you may have and to be an encouragement to you. And lastly
- Search out a Church in the community where you can attend and worship God.

Chapter 14

Bear the Name of God with Pride

The best general definition of the phrase NASA is to "carry" or "bear." The order may merely be better to surrender as follows:

"You shall not bear the name of your God in vain, for God will not hold him guiltless who bears his name in vain," (Exodus 20:7).

If this definition is better, then the way the order alters altogether. The Israelites were separated from others by God himself and called by his name. They bore the name of God before all the world.

This demand turns out to be one that is universal. Because it was God who chose who will bear his name, they should make a mental note that this is not a matter to be taken lightly. They are meant to be a light unto this world, as they bear the name of the LORD.

In this case, the Israelites have unfortunately failed in this task. They bore the name of the LORD in vain.

But that responsibility does not go away. The responsibility falls upon the shoulders of the followers of Christ Jesus since we now bear his wonderful name. Funny how that worked out, uh?

It is out of obedience as well as living a life of holiness that we will bear his name. If we do not take on this responsibility, we will also bear his name in vain.

Do We Bear the Name of Christ?

St. Cyprian and Justina first received the Lord Jesus Christ as their LORD and Savior. They had also been baptized in the name of Jesus, one as a Bishop and the other as a Deaconess and were laboring as missionaries, declaring the mighty acts of the Living God. The same way God inspired Paul by His Divine Grace as "chosen vessels" to bear the Name of our Lord "prior to the Gentiles, and kings, and the children of Israel" (Act 9:15), which in the end led them to their imminent suffering. It is both a blessing and an honor for anyone to "bear the Name of God" as they walk on this earth, to confess the lovely revelation of God's Holy Faith, to spread the zealous preaching of the Godhead, to do your utmost in the wonderful fight of the Truth and Life in Jesus. Not only is it a great honor, but also a great responsibility. When they become impregnated with a child, they take on a great deal of difficulty, taking the pain and the suffering. To bear the name of Jesus, we must do the same, except for a spiritual birth. Our focus as we dedicate our lives to the spiritual works of Christ as we continue to have a watchful eye. This is what it means to bear something. We carry the weight, the burdens, and the difficult sufferings, so much so that it might cost us our lives. It is worth it to me to be able to spend all eternity with God. Therefore, bearing the Name of Christ comes with the greatest responsibility and a challenging call. This becomes so as we bear the Name of Jesus as it means to also bear the Cross for His Name. Your patience and thanksgiving will be tried just for the sake of the Man who bled and died for you. I know mine have. He was crucified on the cross just for you. You must be crucified with him on that cross with him to spend eternity with him. Our Lord and Savior, Jesus Christ was King then and he is still King now. The glory of Christ is His Cross, His Passion. These things are an indication that our journey here on this earth is the one in the same crucifixion and resurrection until we go back to be with him and spend eternal glory with him and can claim the blessings of His Heavenly Kingdom.

However, the question still comes to mind: Do we today bear the Name of God intentionally and without fail? Do we strongly advocate in word and deed the confession of our Holy Accepted Faith so that the Divine righteous joy is conveyed to? These things saith he which hath the sharp majesty with two edges; I know thy works, and where thou dwellest, even where Satan's seat is; and thou holdest fast My Name, and hast not denied My Faith (Revelation 2:12-13).

God's name is the most precious that God, in his love for us humans, has placed in our trust. It holds a wealth beyond measure, and it is something that we hold so dear—our life. It is the glorious self-worth that we receive through Holy Baptism. Have we considered our Divine calling? "Ye were called unto the fellowship of his Son Jesus Christ our Lord" (I Corinthians 1:9). Those who bear the Name of the True Living God first and foremost completely spend their time in fellowship with the Father, the Son, and the Holy Spirit. This is done by the Holy Life of Grace within the established church. We fill the desire of our hearts to be chosen to drink the Spirit of God and become deified: As the Father is the spring (Jeremiah 2:13), and the Son is called a river (Psalm 64:10). We are said to drink the Spirit; for it is written, "We are all made to drink one Spirit," (I Corinthians 12:13). Since we are designed to drink the Spirit, we drink Christ. "For they drank of that spiritual Rock that followed them: and that Rock was Christ,"

(I Corinthians 10:4), (St. Athanasios the Great, Bibliotheke ton Ellenon Pateron kai Ekklesiastikon Syngrapheon, Vol. XXXIII, pp. 107-108).

People were reminded of the wonderful Martyrs Cyprian and Justina on the Feast Day concerning this remarkable reverence and responsibility. We must continuously take a good look at the man or woman in the mirror to examine ourselves to see if we bear the Name of God. We should make sure that we are worthy of beckoning our holy meditations. We are in a position of humbleness and toil, honorable enough to bear the Name of the Father, the Son, and the Holy Spirit. This way, we may be able to secure an eternal life with God's intercessions. Amen.

Concerning the utilization of the name of God, what comparison is there between Christ and those who profess to follow him?

"You are my witnesses," is the utterance of God, "and I am God." (Isa. 43:12). God's greatest Observer, Christ himself deemed it to be an honor to bear the name of the LORD and to make it renowned, (Read Exodus 3:15, John 17: 6, Hebrews 2:12.). As a matter of fact, since Christ declared God's name, he was known as "the Faithful Witness," (Rev. 1:5, Matt.6:9).

The difference is that a lot of people who profess to speak on behalf of God and His Son have demonstrated a dishonorable way of behaving toward the godly, even more so by eliminating it from their usage of the Word of God. Thinking back on a comparable spirit, a current command to Catholic bishops disclosed that, "The name of the LORD in the usage of the Tetragrammaton YHWH is not to be practiced or spoken," for the duration of worship services. How shameful for this type of rationale!

Any More Questions?

Quite a few more questions come up when people think about baptism. The same gift of repentance is given to an individual to start them on the journey of turning from their sins through the process of learning both the truth and unlearning their errors, so an individual must unlearn ordinary false teaching affiliated with baptism. A few of these questions should be viewed.

We should take our first look at ordained ministers. These are the only individuals who are authorized by God to perform baptisms. How important is the spiritual condition, character, and personal beliefs of the person who is performing the baptism?

Let us take a look at John the Baptist, for example. Did he attend any Bible college or theological seminary of his time to become an ordained minister? The answer is no. Still, he baptized many people, including Jesus! This statement is especially important. To be earnest, "Jesus was not a trained ordained minister," either, after the style of the churches of this world. Mostly, the people usually rejected Him and were disliked by the religious hierarchy and leadership of his period. He was littered, persecuted, criticized, and even hated by the leaders during the time He was here on earth. The Bible says that the people many times sought to kill Him. Only because the people did not recognize Him as the Son of God and because He did not compromise with or conform to their sinful ways.

When the Ethiopian eunuch was baptized in Acts 8, Philip, who baptized him, was still a deacon. Philip did become an evangelist in time only after this account (Acts 21:8). It has been explained how Christ's disciples baptized a lot of people. Not any of His disciples were ordained when they performed this baptism. They had been baptized; however, they did not have the Holy Spirit of God. Unlike John and Christ, they had not been converted!

We have also explained how Christ is the one who is placing you into His Church. To immerse means to put into. Christ is immersing you into his body, his Church, at a point in time of baptism! After the 3,000 were baptized on the first Pentecostal of the New Testament Church, Acts says, "And the Lord added to his Church; it was not the ministers who performed the baptisms each day. You can now see that baptism is not the work of an instrument of man. This operation is of Jesus Christ," (Col. 2:12). The instrument of man is not the critical factor in the ordinance of baptism.

Do not watch men, only watch Christ and do not take your eyes from Him! Men will fall to the wayside. They deceive people, sin, or carry out the baptism because they want to get the glorification that God deserves. These things are relevant to Christ's choice to put you into the Church that has been built by him. Learning about the sins, deception, or the intent of the person who baptized you after you have been baptized, you cannot cancel out your baptism and it will not do anything if someone questions you on whether or not your baptism is real or fake because of it. No man can order you to be baptized again. If they could, you could be going through baptism repeatedly until you find someone who is worthy enough to execute it. I can tell you that I have had people who would tell me after I moved away from home that in order for me to join their church, I would have to be baptized again by them. I would tell them no, thank you. Then I replied, the Bible says it is only one baptism, so I refuse to be baptized again. I was baptized by Holy hands. I am not alone. There are others. They want me to be baptized again. How long would it be before you become confused or completely certain that the next pastor would ever turn their back on the Heavenly Father for some unknown reason,

It is not found anywhere in the Bible concerning the possession of the type of supreme divine insight that would be required to correctly discern who can or cannot take to the water to be baptized. Judas was one of the disciples who were baptized on behalf of Christ! When he later went bad and his betrayal eliminated the baptism, he carried it out. No, it did not!

Secondly, a person could always ask, who could perform a baptism? It has already been established that deacons can also perform baptisms and that Christ allowed his disciples who were not yet converted or ordained to execute many baptisms. The term disciple means students and Jesus authorized them the power to heal the sick, raise the dead, cast out demons in his name, preach the gospel of the Kingdom of God, all while they were still not converted (Matt. 10:7-8). However, it was still Jesus who authorized them to do so. The disciples carried out his commission on His behalf while they preached the gospel of the Kingdom of God, which is still on its way. It was never about them being perfect or being ordained that was important.

Acts say when executing baptism in Samaria, Philip, as well, executed miracles and cast out demons while he preached the gospel of the Kingdom of God. Peter and John came at a later time to Samaria, so it is apparent that Philip was not performing on his own authority or without being sent. The apostle probably sent him on ahead because we read in verse 14 upon hearing of many conversions by Philip, the apostle who sent Peter and John to Samaria. The term deacon is a person who "waits" tables (Acts 6:2-3).

The New Testament does put a whole lot of emphasis on the specific individual who is executing the baptism. Still, the pattern is always that the individual who performs the baptism is a representative sent or authorized by a senior pastor or elder, who may or may not have been able to make the trip themselves. These pastors would be a part of the true church of God.

Third, while attempting to deny the necessity for baptism, you will have those who attempt to exercise "the thief on the cross" to prove a point that everyone does not need to be baptized to be saved. Is this true? At this point, it should be perfectly clear that baptism is a biblical command.

Besides, the thief on the cross was a representation of unusual circumstances. He was in a position to obey the command to be baptized. It would not have been unattainable. It is not the actual performance of baptism that redeems us. Instead, it is the forgiveness of Christ and the removal of the death penalty that is over us, by him making us righteous by way of accessing the Holy Spirit and our made-up mind to abide in him in circumstances that can be controlled by us, that does this. It is not for us to worry or be the least bit concerned about the things we cannot control. The Heavenly Father is a merciful God and he always looks at what is on the heart of man, the behavior of an individual.

Always remember that baptism really is a biblical command. Any person who can be baptized should worry and be concerned about their deliverance. If they are ignoring this command. God is commanding everyone all over the world to "repent" (Acts 17:30), and "The Lord is not slack concerning his promise; as some men count slackness; but longsuffering to us-ward, not willing that any should perish, but that all should come to repentance" (II Peter 3:9). These are simple commands that come straight from God. Neglecting or rebelling against God's commands would end an individual's chances for deliverance.

Fourth, should children be baptized? Many people attend the many popular "Christian" churches on this earth. Baptizing babies and children is a practice that is all too common in the churches. The problem with that is this, it is not biblical! But why?

People should consider the following viewpoints. There is not a place in the Bible that records the baptism of a child. No, not one when Philip was performing a baptism. Acts 8:12 says, "They were baptized, both men and women." There is no mention of him baptizing any children in this account. Children are not mature enough to begin to understand what baptism is all about.

The Word commands us to "repent and believe." Infants and young children are not capable of believing or even comprehending the true gospel of God's Kingdom. They cannot understand a huge world-ruling Kingdom led by Christ and the resurrection of the saints of God, coming to do away with the world's government and replace it with the Kingdom of God. This is too much for a child to begin to handle or understand. Can a child truly comprehend that Christ died upon the cross for their sins? Is a child capable enough to comprehend the symbolism of the death, burial, and resurrection of Christ and how it corresponds to the baptism ceremony? Can a child understand accepting the Spirit of God as understanding in the mind?

Babies have no reason to repent, on the other hand, young individuals have for sure done a lot of things that they could, at least partially, see were unrighteous. It is true that children are capable of short-term, limited feelings of sorrow or guilt. However, they are quickly forgotten in the relaxed world of a child's life. Children are so quick to wander off into their own little world and do other things. I have not ever seen a case where a child had the capability of understanding the definition of baptism and I have ministered to a lot of people for over 25 years. Children are likely to endure a commitment that is involved in becoming a true follower of Christ Jesus, such as having a boyfriend or girlfriend or being married-that they might have in their young lives.

While some teenagers might grow up quicker than others, most individuals do not reach true adult maturity until they are at least in their early twenties. At the age of 18, which is the minimum age at which an individual has the capability of understanding the meaning of baptism. If you are a young person and you are reading this book, give yourself some time to grow and develop and you are without a doubt and are really sure that you know what you are doing and what is at stake in the decision you are to make to become a Christian. And yes, adults should not hesitate to reach repentance, but young people should wait, often believing a few years before taking this step of baptism.

When the holier-than-thou, sanctimonious Pharisees came to John the Baptist to be baptized, he told them, "Bring forth fruits worthy of repentance," (Luke 3:8). They all were adults. Young people as well are required to bring forth fruits worthy of repentance. This is not said because young individuals are self-deceptive. However, instead they require time to realize their own trustworthiness and belief expand. Young individuals really need to know deep down inside themselves without any doubt whatsoever that they have repented. Otherwise, they will not have the certainty they will later know that God has already given them His Holy Spirit. Our journey that we travel on the path to God's Kingdom will require that we know without any doubt that we have the Spirit of God in us, assisting us in a time of need!

Counseling For Baptism

We should take into account the struggle that rose up in the church at Corinth concerning which apostle the brethren in the church should follow. Take note, I Cor. 1:13-17, "Is Christ divided? Was Paul crucified for you? Even so, were you baptized in Paul's name?" I truly thank God that I did not baptize no one of you, but Crispus and Gaius, lest any should say that I had baptized in my own name. And I baptized also the household of Stephanas: besides, I know not whether I baptized any other. For Christ sent me not to baptize, but to preach the gospel.

In addition, I cannot, not me personally, baptize individuals that are in all parts of the Earth. Paul had representatives who "stood" in for Paul and carried out baptisms that were ready to happen. Yet, it is not important that I baptize you directly. I also do not desire anyone to see me in any type of special way for the reason that has already been explained earlier. It is Jesus who places you into his Church, not me or any other man! Even if I could baptize you directly and I have baptized a few people in my lifetime, I would only still be performing it as a servant of Christ, acting on His behalf, not on my own. While the representatives are all around the Earth, they perform everything in their power, with the assistance of God, to work out a way to reach you. If the

Father is calling you, He will also make a way for you to be baptized. You can completely believe in this!

An essential viewpoint: A few people will get in touch with a belief they are already true Christians- that the Holy Spirit is already leading them. However, they lack the correct baptism. They are simply searching for someone to baptize them to crucify an artificial conversion. Understanding this, without having a great understanding of the doctrines from the Bible, true repentance, or knowledge of conversion—all of this with a proper baptism—one is not a real

Christian and we cannot baptize. You must "Work out your own salvation with fear and trembling, " (Phil. 2:12). You must "count the cost" (Luke 14:25-30) and make the decision whether you will make up your mind and answer God's call.

BAPTISM SYMBOLS
Baptism is recognized as one of the earliest and most prevalent of Christian rites. Although the idea did not originate with Christianity, it has been practiced by nearly all major Christian denominations throughout the centuries.
BAPTISMAL FONT
DOVE
CROSS
CANDLE
WATER
OIL
SEASHELL
ICHTHYS
FLAME
BAPTISM GARMENT
CHI-RHO
symbolsage.com

BIBLIOGRAPHY

All About God, 2002-2017 http://www.allaboutgod.com/what-is-a-christian.htm

Beyond Today United Church of God, an International Association, Apr 20, 2012 https://www.ucg.org/bible-study-tools/booklets/transforming-your-life-the-process-of-conversion/introduction

How much influence does Satan Have over my Thoughts?

How much influence does Satan have over my thoughts? (churchofjesuschrist.org)

Deuteronomy 30:19

https://www.bing.com/search?q=god+does+not+force+himself+on+us+bible+verse&qs=NM&pq

Batty, David, Renewing Your Mind, The Challenge of Renewing Your Mind, Living Free, Discovering God's Path to Freedom

http://www.livingfree.org/index.php?option=com content&view=article&id=593:renewing-your-mind&catid=80:life-controlling-problems&Itemid=187

Bibleinfro.com http://www.bibleinfo.com/en/questions/armor-of-god#bel

Bible Line Ministries, http://www.biblelineministries.org/articles/basearch.php3?action=full&mainkey=BE+CONVERTED

Cole, Steven J. Lesson 2: When God Brings Revival (Luke 1:5-17) June 2013 https://bible.org/seriespage/lesson-2-when-god-brings-revival-luke-15-17

Gospel, Fundamental, Chapter 17, The Church of Latter-Day Saints, Salt Lake City, Utah 1992, 2002

LeClaire, Jennifer, Are You a True Follower of Christ? Really? The Plum Line April 2012

http://www.charismamag.com/blogs/the-plumb-line/15063-are-you-a-true-follower-of-christ-reall

† Metropolitan Cyprian of Oropos and Fili *Source: Ἅγιος Κυπριανός, No. 232 (September-October 1989), pp. 89-90. Proudly Bear God's Name

On the Commemoration of Sts. Cyprian and Justina (2 October) NewSpring Church, What does Baptism Mean?

https://newspring.cc/studies/going-public-a-7-day-study-about-baptism-and-why-it-matters/what-does-baptism-mean

Kirby, Peter, Pliny the Younger, Early Christian Writing, 2001-2017 http://www.earlychristianwritings.com/text/pliny.html

LeClaire, Jennifer, Are You a True Follower of Christ? Really? The Plum Line April 2012

http://www.charismamag.com/blogs/the-plumb-line/15063-are-you-a-true-follower-of-christ-reall

Explore God https://www.exploregod.com/how-can-i-grow-spiritually

† Metropolitan Cyprian of Oropos and Fili *Source: Ἅγιος Κυπριανός, No. 232 (September-October 1989), pp. 89-90. Proudly Bear God's Name...

On the Commemoration of Sts. Cyprian and Justina (2 October)

Myers, Joyer How to Live for God Not Your Feelings

https://bible.org/illustration/how-live-god

NewSpring Church, What Does Baptism Mean?

https://newspring.cc/studies/going-public-a-7-day-study-about-baptism-and-why-it-matters/what-does-baptism-meanhttps://www.exploregod.com/enhttps://www.exploregod.com/en

St. Athanasios the Great, Bibliotheke ton Ellenon Pateron kai Ekklesiastikon Syngrapheon, Vol. XXXIII, pp. 107-108).

Schneider, Wolfgang,Praying with the right attitude http://www.biblecenter.de/bibel/studien/e-std015.php

University of Minnesota https://www.takingcharge.csh.umn.edu/what-spirituality

https://www.ligonier.org/learn/articles/what-true-conversion, Dr. Steven J. Lawson

https://www.biblestudytools.com/dictionaries/bakers-evangelical-dictionary/convert-conversion.html...Darrell L. Bock

Transforming Your Life /The Process of Conversion - Roger Foster, Scott Ashley Tom Robinson

What do you Mean "Water Baptism"? David C. Peck

What is True Conversion? - David C. Peck

https://haynes.com/en-us/tips-tutorials/what-wheel-alignment-and-what-does-it-do

Alignment With God - What It Means and Looks Like | Jenn Schultz (jennschultzauthor.com)

https://www.lovetoknow.com/parenting/baby/baptism-symbols/ Dr. Vilma Ruddock,M.D

https://www.lovetoknow.com/parenting/baby/baptism-symbols/Father Michael Van Sloun

https://symbolsage.com/baptism-symbols-history/ Nemanja